**HBR'S
10
MUST
READS**

On
Mental
Toughness

HBR's 10 Must Reads series is the definitive collection of ideas and best practices for aspiring and experienced leaders alike. These books offer essential reading selected from the pages of *Harvard Business Review* on topics critical to the success of every manager.

Titles include:

On
Mental
Toughness

HARVARD BUSINESS REVIEW PRESS
Boston, Massachusetts

Copyright 2018 Harvard Business School Publishing Corporation
All rights reserved
Printed in the United States of America
20 19 18 17 16 15 14 13 12 11

The web addresses referenced in this book were live and correct at the time of the book's publication but may be subject to change.

Cataloging-in-Publication data forthcoming

ISBN: 978-1-63369-436-1
eISBN: 978-1-63369-437-8

The paper used in this publication meets the requirements of the American National Standard for Permanence of Paper for Publications and Documents in Libraries and Archives Z39.48-1992.

Contents

On
Mental Toughness

How the Best of the Best Get Better and Better

by Graham Jones

UNTIL 1954, MOST PEOPLE BELIEVED that a human being was incapable of running a mile in less than four minutes. But that very year, English miler Roger Bannister proved them wrong.

"Doctors and scientists said that breaking the four-minute mile was impossible, that one would die in the attempt," Bannister is reported to have said afterward. "Thus, when I got up from the track after collapsing at the finish line, I figured I was dead." Which goes to show that in sports, as in business, the main obstacle to achieving "the impossible" may be a self-limiting mind-set.

As a sports psychologist, I spent much of my career as a consultant to Olympic and world champions in rowing, swimming, squash, track and field, sailing, trampolining, and judo. Then in 1995, I teamed up with Olympic gold medal swimmer Adrian Moorhouse to start Lane4, a firm that has been bringing the lessons from elite athletic performance to *Fortune* 500 and FTSE 100 companies, with the help of other world-class athletes such as Greg Searle, Alison Mowbray, and Tom Murray. Sport is not business, of course, but the parallels are striking. In both worlds, elite performers are not born but made. Obviously, star athletes must have some innate, natural ability—coordination, physical flexibility, anatomical capacities—just as successful senior executives need to be able to think strategically and relate to people. But the real key to excellence in both sports and business is not the ability to swim fast or do quantitative analyses quickly in your head; rather, it is mental toughness.

Elite performers in both arenas thrive on pressure; they excel when the heat is turned up. Their rise to the top is the result of very careful planning—of setting and hitting hundreds of small goals. Elite performers use competition to hone their skills, and they reinvent themselves continually to stay ahead of the pack. Finally, whenever they score big wins, top performers take time to celebrate their victories. Let's look at how these behaviors translate to the executive suite.

Love the Pressure

You can't stay at the top if you aren't comfortable in high-stress situations. Indeed, the ability to remain cool under fire is the one trait of elite performers that is most often thought of as inborn. But in fact you can learn to love the pressure—for driving you to perform better than you ever thought you could. To do that, however, you have to first make a *choice* to devote yourself passionately to self-improvement. Greg Searle, who won an Olympic gold medal in rowing, is often asked whether success was worth the price. He always gives the same reply: "I never made any sacrifices; I made choices."

Managing pressure is a lot easier if you can focus just on your own excellence. Top sports performers don't allow themselves to be distracted by the victories or failures of others. They concentrate on what they can control and forget the rest. They rarely let themselves be sidetracked by events outside a competition. World-class golfer Darren Clarke, for example, helped lead the European team to a Ryder Cup victory in 2006, six weeks after the death of his beloved wife. Elite performers are masters of compartmentalization.

If you want to be a high flier in business, you must be equally inner-focused and self-directed. Consider one executive I'll call Jack. When he was a young man, wrestling was his passion, and he turned down an offer from Harvard to attend a less-prominent undergraduate school that had a better-ranked wrestling team. Later, after earning his MBA, Jack was recruited by a prestigious investment-banking firm, where he eventually rose up to the rank of executive director. Even then, he wasn't driven by any need to impress others. "Don't think for a minute I'm doing this for the status," he once told me. "I'm doing it for myself. This is the stuff I think about in the shower. I'd do it even if I didn't earn a penny."

People who are as self-motivated as Jack or Darren Clarke rarely indulge in self-flagellation. That's not to say that elite performers aren't hard on themselves; they would not have gotten so far without being hard on themselves. But when things go awry, business and sports superstars dust themselves off and move on.

Another thing that helps star performers love the pressure is their ability to switch their involvement in their endeavors on and off. A good way to do this is to have a secondary passion in life. Rower Alison Mowbray, for example, always set time aside to practice the piano, despite her grueling athletic-training schedule. Not only did she win a silver medal in the Olympics in 2004, but she also became an accomplished pianist in the process.

For top executives, the adrenaline rush of the job can be so addictive that it's difficult to break away. But unless you are able to put the day behind you, as elite athletes can, you'll inevitably run the risk of burning out. Many leading businesspeople are passionate about their hobbies; Richard Branson is famous for his hot-air balloon adventures, for instance. However, even small diversions such as bridge or the opera can be remarkably powerful in helping executives tune out and reenergize.

Fixate on the Long Term

Much of star athletes' ability to rebound from defeat comes from an intense focus on long-term goals and aspirations. At the same time, both sports stars and their coaches are keenly aware that the road to long-term success is paved with small achievements.

The trick here is to meticulously plan short-term goals so that performance will peak at major, rather than minor, events. For athletes who participate in Olympic sports, for example, the training and preparation are geared to a four-year cycle. However, these athletes may also be competing in world championships every year. The inevitable tension arising from this complicated timetable requires very careful management.

Adrian Moorhouse's Olympic gold medal success in 1988 is a case in point. His long-term goal was to swim the 100-meter breaststroke in a time of 62 seconds, because he and his coach had calculated four years in advance that this time should be good enough to win the gold. Of course, Adrian thought about winning in the interim, but all of his training and practice was geared toward hitting a time of 62 seconds or better in the Summer Olympics in Seoul. He mapped out specific short-term goals in every area that would affect his performance—strength training, nutrition, mental toughness, technique and more—to make sure he achieved that ultimate goal.

Successful executives often carefully plan out their path to a long-term goal too. I once coached a woman I'll call Deborah, an IT manager who worked for a low-budget airline. Her long-term goal was to become a senior executive in three years. To that end, we identified several performance areas in which she needed to excel—for example, increasing her reputation and influence among executives in other departments of the company and managing complex initiatives. We then identified short-term goals that underpinned achievements in each performance area, such as joining a companywide task force and leading an international project. Together we built a system that closely monitored whether Deborah was achieving the interim goals that would help her fulfill her long-term vision. It paid off. Two months short of her three-year target, Deborah was offered an opportunity to head up the $12 million in-flight business sales unit.

Use the Competition

It's common in track-and-field sports for two elite athletes from different countries to train together. I was at a pre-1996 Olympics training camp for the British team where 100-meter sprinter and then current Olympic champion Linford Christie had a "guest" train with him. His training partner just happened to be Namibian Frankie Fredericks, a silver medalist who had been one of the major threats to Christie's Olympic crown.

World champion rower Tom Murray told me just how competing with the best inspired him to higher achievement. Murray was part of a group of 40 rowers selected to train together with the hopes of gaining one of the 14 spots on the 1996 U.S. Olympic rowing team. Because the final team was chosen only two months before the Atlanta games, this meant that the group of 40 trained together for almost four years.

As Murray recalled, one of the last performance evaluations during the final week leading up to the naming of the Olympic team involved a 2,000-meter test on the rowing machine. The 40 athletes took it in four waves of 10; Murray went in the third wave. During the first two waves, 15 rowers set personal best times, and two recorded times that were faster than anyone in the U.S. had ever gone. The benchmark was immediately raised. Murray realized that he needed to row faster than he'd anticipated. He ended up bettering his previous personal best by three seconds and subsequently made the 1996 team.

If you hope to make it to the very top, like Murray, you too will need to make sure you "train" with the people who will push you the hardest. I once coached an executive I'll call Karl. He declined an opportunity to take a position as the second-in-command at a competitor's firm at twice his current salary. Karl passed up what looked like a standout career opportunity because his current company was deeply committed to coaching him and a cohort of other senior executives on how to become better leaders. Karl had a reputation for burning people out, and he realized that if he moved on, he would continue that pattern of behavior. He remained in the same job because he knew that his coach and peers would help him grow and change his ways.

Smart companies consciously create situations in which their elite performers push one another to levels they would never reach if they were working with less-accomplished colleagues. Talent development programs that bring together a company's stars for intensive training often serve precisely such a purpose. If you want to become a world-class executive, getting into such a program should be one of your first goals.

Reinvent Yourself

It's hard enough getting to the top, but staying there is even harder. You've won that Olympic medal or broken that world record or racked up more wins than anyone in your sport. So how do you motivate yourself to embark on another cycle of building the mental and physical endurance required to win the next time, especially now that you have become the benchmark? That is one of the most difficult challenges facing elite performers, who have to keep reinventing themselves.

Consider trampolinist Sue Shotton. I was working with her when she achieved the number one ranking among women in 1983—that is, she was considered to be the best female trampolinist in the world. Yet she had still not won a world championship.

Shotton was determined to capture that title, and she left nothing to chance. She challenged herself constantly by working with specialists such as physiologists, biomechanists, and elite sports coaches who kept her up to date on cutting-edge thinking. She perfected new moves based on video analysis; she tried different ways of boosting her energy based on nutritional intake. Her efforts to find ways of staying ahead of fiercely ambitious competitors paid off when she won the world championship in 1984, becoming the first British woman ever to hold the title.

Shotton had an insatiable appetite for feedback—a quality I have seen in all the top business performers I have worked with. They have a particularly strong need for instant, in the moment feedback. One top sales and marketing director I worked with told me that he would never have stayed at his current position if the CEO hadn't given him relentless, sometimes brutally honest critiques.

If you're like the elite business performers I have coached, you too are hungry for advice on how to develop and progress. One word of caution, however: While it's good to feel challenged, you need to make sure that any feedback you get is constructive. If criticism doesn't seem helpful at first, probe to see if you can get useful insights about what's behind the negative feedback. Get more specifics. You should be able to see concrete improvements in your performance after getting detailed coaching advice.

Celebrate the Victories

Elite performers know how to party—indeed, they put almost as much effort into their celebrations as they do into their accomplishments. I once worked with a professional golfer who, as he worked his way up the ranks to the top of his sport, would reward himself with something he had prized as a young player—an expensive watch, a fancy car, a new home. These were reminders of his achievements and symbolized to him the hard work, commitment, and dedication he had put into golf for so many years.

Celebration is more than an emotional release. Done effectively, it involves a deep level of analysis and enhanced awareness. The very best performers do not move on before they have scrutinized and understood thoroughly the factors underpinning their success. I saw that discipline in the Welsh rugby team, which I advised from 2000 to 2002. After each game, the team members made a special effort to highlight not only what they did poorly but what they did particularly well. They typically split into small groups to identify and discuss the positive aspects of their performance, so that they could focus on reproducing them in the next game. The exercise was a powerful way to build expertise—and self-confidence. Indeed, the most important function of affirming victory is to provide encouragement for attempts at even tougher stretch goals.

In business, where companies are pressed to meet quarterly earnings and stockholders are impatient, managers must consider the timing and duration of the celebration. Dwelling on success for too long is a distraction and, worse, leads to complacency. Celebrate—but push on. Don't get stuck in the rituals of success. At the end of the day, getting to the next level of performance is what celebrating is really all about.

Smart companies know how to manage the tension between celebrating and looking hungrily for their next achievement. One UK mobile telecom provider puts on an annual ball for its people—spending over £1 million a year. The company hires out well-known venues and brings in pop bands to entertain all the employees. But one factor in the company's success is that its managers know that partying comes number nine on the list of top 10 reasons for wanting to win. Like all elite performers, they also know that partying must be deserved. Without victory, celebrations are meaningless.

The Will to Win

As the spectacle of the Olympics unfolds, it will be easy to be captivated by the flawless performance of elite athletes who make their accomplishments seem almost effortless. Such effortlessness is an illusion, though. Even the most youthful star has typically put in countless years of preparation and has endured repeated failures. But what drives all these elite performers is a fierce desire to compete—and win. Even so, most of those participating in the Olympics this summer will walk away from the games without grabbing a single medal. Those with real mettle will get back into training again. That's what truly separates elite performers from ordinary high achievers. It takes supreme, almost unimaginable grit and courage to get back into the ring and fight to the bitter end. That's what the Olympic athlete does. If you want to be an elite performer in business, that's what you need to do, too.

Originally published in June 2008. Reprint R0806H

Crucibles of Leadership

by Warren G. Bennis and Robert J. Thomas

AS LIFELONG STUDENTS OF LEADERSHIP, we are fascinated with the notion of what makes a leader. Why is it that certain people seem to naturally inspire confidence, loyalty, and hard work, while others (who may have just as much vision and smarts) stumble, again and again? It's a timeless question, and there's no simple answer. But we have come to believe it has something to do with the different ways that people deal with adversity. Indeed, our recent research has led us to conclude that one of the most reliable indicators and predictors of true leadership is an individual's ability to find meaning in negative events and to learn from even the most trying circumstances. Put another way, the skills required to conquer adversity and emerge stronger and more committed than ever are the same ones that make for extraordinary leaders.

Take Sidney Harman. Thirty-four years ago, the then-48-year-old businessman was holding down two executive positions. He was the chief executive of Harman Kardon (now Harman International), the audio components company he had cofounded, and he was serving as president of Friends World College, now Friends World Program, an experimental Quaker school on Long Island whose essential philosophy is that students, not their teachers, are responsible for their education. Juggling the two jobs, Harman was living what he calls a "bifurcated life," changing clothes in his car and eating lunch as he drove between Harman Kardon offices and plants and the Friends

World campus. One day while at the college, he was told his company's factory in Bolivar, Tennessee, was having a crisis.

He immediately rushed to the Bolivar factory, a facility that was, as Harman now recalls, "raw, ugly, and, in many ways, demeaning." The problem, he found, had erupted in the polish and buff department, where a crew of a dozen workers, mostly African-Americans, did the dull, hard work of polishing mirrors and other parts, often under unhealthy conditions. The men on the night shift were supposed to get a coffee break at 10 p.m. When the buzzer that announced the workers' break went on the fritz, management arbitrarily decided to postpone the break for ten minutes, when another buzzer was scheduled to sound. But one worker, "an old black man with an almost biblical name, Noah B. Cross," had "an epiphany," as Harman describes it. "He said, literally, to his fellow workers, 'I don't work for no buzzer. The buzzer works for me. It's my job to tell me when it's ten o'clock. I got me a watch. I'm not waiting another ten minutes. I'm going on my coffee break.' And all 12 guys took their coffee break, and, of course, all hell broke loose."

The worker's principled rebellion—his refusal to be cowed by management's senseless rule—was, in turn, a revelation to Harman: "The technology is there to serve the men, not the reverse," he remembers realizing. "I suddenly had this awakening that everything I was doing at the college had appropriate applications in business." In the ensuing years, Harman revamped the factory and its workings, turning it into a kind of campus—offering classes on the premises, including piano lessons, and encouraging the workers to take most of the responsibility for running their workplace. Further, he created an environment where dissent was not only tolerated but also encouraged. The plant's lively independent newspaper, the *Bolivar Mirror*, gave workers a creative and emotional outlet—and they enthusiastically skewered Harman in its pages.

Harman had, unexpectedly, become a pioneer of participative management, a movement that continues to influence the shape of workplaces around the world. The concept wasn't a grand idea conceived in the CEO's office and imposed on the plant, Harman says. It grew organically out of his going down to Bolivar to, in his words,

Idea in Brief

What enables one leader to inspire confidence, loyalty, and hard work, while others—with equal vision and intelligence—stumble? How individuals deal with adversity provides a clue.

Extraordinary leaders find meaning in—and learn from—the most negative events. Like phoenixes

rising from the ashes, they emerge from adversity stronger, more confident in themselves and their purpose, and more committed to their work.

Such transformative events are called **crucibles**—a severe test or trial. Crucibles are intense, often traumatic—and always unplanned.

"put out this fire." Harman's transformation was, above all, a creative one. He had connected two seemingly unrelated ideas and created a radically different approach to management that recognized both the economic and humane benefits of a more collegial workplace. Harman went on to accomplish far more during his career. In addition to founding Harman International, he served as the deputy secretary of commerce under Jimmy Carter. But he always looked back on the incident in Bolivar as the formative event in his professional life, the moment he came into his own as a leader.

The details of Harman's story are unique, but their significance is not. In interviewing more than 40 top leaders in business and the public sector over the past three years, we were surprised to find that all of them—young and old—were able to point to intense, often traumatic, always unplanned experiences that had transformed them and had become the sources of their distinctive leadership abilities.

We came to call the experiences that shape leaders "crucibles," after the vessels medieval alchemists used in their attempts to turn base metals into gold. For the leaders we interviewed, the crucible experience was a trial and a test, a point of deep self-reflection that forced them to question who they were and what mattered to them. It required them to examine their values, question their assumptions, hone their judgment. And, invariably, they emerged from the crucible stronger and more sure of themselves and their purpose— changed in some fundamental way.

Idea in Practice

The Crucible Experience

Crucibles force leaders into deep self-reflection, where they examine their values, question their assumptions, and hone their judgment.

Example: Sidney Harman—co-founder of audio components company Harman Kardon and president of an experimental college encouraging student-driven education—encountered his crucible when "all hell broke loose" in one of his factories. After managers postponed a scheduled break because the buzzer didn't sound, workers rebelled. "I don't work for no buzzer," one proclaimed.

To Harman, this refusal to bow to management's senseless rule suggested a surprising link between student-driven education and business. Pioneering participative management, Harman transformed his plant into a kind of campus, offering classes and encouraging dissent. He considers the rebellion the formative event in his career—the moment he became a true leader.

The Many Shapes of Crucibles

Some crucibles are violent and life-threatening (encounters with prejudice, illness); others are more positive, yet profoundly challenging (such as demanding bosses or mentors). Whatever the shape, leaders create a narrative telling how they met the challenge and became better for it.

Example: While working for former Atlanta mayor Robert F. Maddox, Vernon Jordan endured repeated racial heckling from Maddox. Rather than letting Maddox's sadism destroy him, Jordan interpreted the be-

Leadership crucibles can take many forms. Some are violent, life-threatening events. Others are more prosaic episodes of self-doubt. But whatever the crucible's nature, the people we spoke with were able, like Harman, to create a narrative around it, a story of how they were challenged, met the challenge, and became better leaders. As we studied these stories, we found that they not only told us how individual leaders are shaped but also pointed to some characteristics that seem common to all leaders—characteristics that were formed, or at least exposed, in the crucible.

havior as a desperate lashing out by someone who knew the era of the Old South was ending. Jordan's response empowered him to become an esteemed lawyer and presidential advisor.

Essential Leadership Skills

Four skills enable leaders to learn from adversity:

1. **Engage others in shared meaning.** For example, Sidney Harman mobilized employees around a radical new management approach—amid a factory crisis.

2. **A distinctive, compelling voice.** With words alone, college president Jack Coleman preempted a violent clash between the football team and anti-Vietnam War demonstrators threatening to burn the American flag. Coleman's suggestion to the protestors? Lower the flag, wash it, then put it back up.

3. **Integrity.** Coleman's values prevailed during the emotionally charged face-off between antiwar demonstrators and irate football players.

4. **Adaptive capacity.** This most critical skill includes the *ability to grasp context*, and *hardiness*. Grasping context requires weighing many factors (e.g., how different people will interpret a gesture). Without this quality, leaders can't connect with constituents.

Hardiness provides the perseverance and toughness needed to remain hopeful despite disaster. For instance, Michael Klein made millions in real estate during his teens, lost it all by age 20—then built several more businesses, including transforming a tiny software company into a Hewlett-Packard acquisition.

Learning from Difference

A crucible is, by definition, a transformative experience through which an individual comes to a new or an altered sense of identity. It is perhaps not surprising then that one of the most common types of crucibles we documented involves the experience of prejudice. Being a victim of prejudice is particularly traumatic because it forces an individual to confront a distorted picture of him- or herself, and it often unleashes profound feelings of anger, bewilderment, and even withdrawal. For all its trauma, however, the experience of prejudice is for some a clarifying event. Through it, they gain a clearer vision of who they are, the role they play, and their place in the world.

Consider, for example, Liz Altman, now a Motorola vice president, who was transformed by the year she spent at a Sony camcorder factory in rural Japan, where she faced both estrangement and sexism. It was, says Altman, "by far, the hardest thing I've ever done." The foreign culture—particularly its emphasis on groups over individuals—was both a shock and a challenge to a young American woman. It wasn't just that she felt lonely in an alien world. She had to face the daunting prospect of carving out a place for herself as the only woman engineer in a plant, and nation, where women usually serve as low-level assistants and clerks known as "office ladies."

Another woman who had come to Japan under similar circumstances had warned Altman that the only way to win the men's respect was to avoid becoming allied with the office ladies. But on her very first morning, when the bell rang for a coffee break, the men headed in one direction and the women in another—and the women saved her a place at their table, while the men ignored her. Instinct told Altman to ignore the warning rather than insult the women by rebuffing their invitation.

Over the next few days, she continued to join the women during breaks, a choice that gave her a comfortable haven from which to observe the unfamiliar office culture. But it didn't take her long to notice that some of the men spent the break at their desks reading magazines, and Altman determined that she could do the same on occasion. Finally, after paying close attention to the conversations around her, she learned that several of the men were interested in mountain biking. Because Altman wanted to buy a mountain bike, she approached them for advice. Thus, over time, she established herself as something of a free agent, sometimes sitting with the women and other times engaging with the men.

And as it happened, one of the women she'd sat with on her very first day, the department secretary, was married to one of the engineers. The secretary took it upon herself to include Altman in social gatherings, a turn of events that probably wouldn't have occurred if Altman had alienated her female coworkers on that first day. "Had I just gone to try to break in with [the men] and not had her as an ally, it would never have happened," she says.

Looking back, Altman believes the experience greatly helped her gain a clearer sense of her personal strengths and capabilities, preparing her for other difficult situations. Her tenure in Japan taught her to observe closely and to avoid jumping to conclusions based on cultural assumptions—invaluable skills in her current position at Motorola, where she leads efforts to smooth alliances with other corporate cultures, including those of Motorola's different regional operations.

Altman has come to believe that she wouldn't have been as able to do the Motorola job if she hadn't lived in a foreign country and experienced the dissonance of cultures: ". . . even if you're sitting in the same room, ostensibly agreeing . . . unless you understand the frame of reference, you're probably missing a bunch of what's going on." Altman also credits her crucible with building her confidence—she feels that she can cope with just about anything that comes her way.

People can feel the stigma of cultural differences much closer to home, as well. Muriel ("Mickie") Siebert, the first woman to own a seat on the New York Stock Exchange, found her crucible on the Wall Street of the 1950s and 1960s, an arena so sexist that she couldn't get a job as a stockbroker until she took her first name off her résumé and substituted a genderless initial. Other than the secretaries and the occasional analyst, women were few and far between. That she was Jewish was another strike against her at a time, she points out, when most of big business was "not nice" to either women or Jews. But Siebert wasn't broken or defeated. Instead, she emerged stronger, more focused, and more determined to change the status quo that excluded her.

When we interviewed Siebert, she described her way of addressing anti-Semitism—a technique that quieted the offensive comments of her peers without destroying the relationships she needed to do her job effectively. According to Siebert, at the time it was part of doing business to have a few drinks at lunch. She remembers, "Give somebody a couple of drinks, and they would talk about the Jews." She had a greeting card she used for those occasions that went like this:

Roses are reddish,
Violets are bluish,
In case you don't know,
I am Jewish.

Siebert would have the card hand-delivered to the person who had made the anti-Semitic remarks, and on the card she had written, "Enjoyed lunch." As she recounts, "They got that card in the afternoon, and I never had to take any of that nonsense again. And I never embarrassed anyone, either." It was because she was unable to get credit for the business she was bringing in at any of the large Wall Street firms that she bought a seat on the New York Stock Exchange and started working for herself.

In subsequent years, she went on to found Muriel Siebert & Company (now Siebert Financial Corporation) and has dedicated herself to helping other people avoid some of the difficulties she faced as a young professional. A prominent advocate for women in business and a leader in developing financial products directed at women, she's also devoted to educating children about financial opportunities and responsibility.

We didn't interview lawyer and presidential adviser Vernon Jordan for this article, but he, too, offers a powerful reminder of how prejudice can prove transformational rather than debilitating. In *Vernon Can Read! A Memoir* (Public Affairs, 2001), Jordan describes the vicious baiting he was subjected to as a young man. The man who treated him in this offensive way was his employer, Robert F. Maddox. Jordan served the racist former mayor of Atlanta at dinner, in a white jacket, with a napkin over his arm. He also functioned as Maddox's chauffeur. Whenever Maddox could, he would derisively announce, "Vernon can read!" as if the literacy of a young African-American were a source of wonderment.

Geeks and Geezers

WE DIDN'T SET OUT TO LEARN about crucibles. Our research for this article and for our new book, *Geeks and Geezers*, was actually designed to uncover the ways that *era* influences a leader's motivation and aspirations. We interviewed 43 of today's top leaders in business and the public sector, limiting our subjects to people born in or before 1925, or in or after 1970. To our delight, we learned a lot about how age and era affect leadership style.

Our geeks and geezers (the affectionate shorthand we eventually used to describe the two groups) had very different ideas about paying your dues, work-life balance, the role of heroes, and more. But they also shared some striking similarities—among them a love of learning and strong sense of values. Most intriguing, though, both our geeks and our geezers told us again and again how certain experiences inspired them, shaped them, and, indeed, taught them to lead. And so, as the best research often does, our work turned out to be even more interesting than we thought it would be. We continued to explore the influences of era—our findings are described in our book—but at the same time we probed for stories of these crucible experiences. These are the stories we share with you here.

Subjected to this type of abuse, a lesser man might have allowed Maddox to destroy him. But in his memoir, Jordan gives his own interpretation of Maddox's sadistic heckling, a tale that empowered Jordan instead of embittering him. When he looked at Maddox through the rearview mirror, Jordan did not see a powerful member of Georgia's ruling class. He saw a desperate anachronism, a person who lashed out because he knew his time was up. As Jordan writes about Maddox, "His half-mocking, half-serious comments about my education were the death rattle of his culture. When he saw that I was . . . crafting a life for myself that would make me a man in . . . ways he thought of as being a man, he was deeply unnerved."

Maddox's cruelty was the crucible that, consciously or not, Jordan imbued with redemptive meaning. Instead of lashing out or being paralyzed with hatred, Jordan saw the fall of the Old South and imagined his own future freed of the historical shackles of racism. His ability to organize meaning around a potential crisis turned it into the crucible around which his leadership was forged.

Reinvention in the Extreme:
The Power of Neoteny

ALL OF OUR INTERVIEW SUBJECTS described their crucibles as opportunities for reinvention—for taking stock of their lives and finding meaning in circumstances many people would see as daunting and potentially incapacitating. In the extreme, this capacity for reinvention comes to resemble eternal youth—a kind of vigor, openness, and an enduring capacity for wonder that is the antithesis of stereotyped old age.

We borrowed a term from biology—"neoteny," which, according to the *American Heritage Dictionary*, means "retention of juvenile characteristics in the adults of a species"—to describe this quality, this delight in lifelong learning, which every leader we interviewed displayed, regardless of age. To a person, they were full of energy, curiosity, and confidence that the world is a place of wonders spread before them like an endless feast.

Robert Galvin, former Motorola chairman now in his late 70s, spends his weekends windsurfing. Arthur Levitt Jr., former SEC chairman who turned 71 this year, is an avid Outward Bound trekker. And architect Frank Gehry is now a 72-year-old ice hockey player. But it's not only an affinity for physical activity that characterizes neoteny—it's an appetite for learning and self-development, a curiosity and passion for life.

To understand why this quality is so powerful in a leader, it might help to take a quick look at the scientific principle behind it—neoteny as an evolutionary engine. It is the winning, puppyish quality of certain ancient wolves that allowed them to evolve into dogs. Over thousands of years, humans favored wolves that were the friendliest, most approachable, and most curious. Naturally, people were most drawn to the wolves least likely to attack without warning, that readily locked eyes with them, and that seemed almost human in their eager response to people; the ones, in short, that stayed the most like puppies. Like human infants, they have certain physical qualities that elicit a nurturing response in human adults.

Prevailing over Darkness

Some crucible experiences illuminate a hidden and suppressed area of the soul. These are often among the harshest of crucibles, involving, for instance, episodes of illness or violence. In the case of Sidney Rittenberg, now 79, the crucible took the form of 16 years of unjust imprisonment, in solitary confinement, in Communist China. In

When infants see an adult, they often respond with a smile that begins small and slowly grows into a radiant grin that makes the adult feel at center of the universe. Recent studies of bonding indicate that nursing and other intimate interactions with an infant cause the mother's system to be flooded with oxytocin, a calming, feel-good hormone that is a powerful antidote to cortisol, the hormone produced by stress. Oxytocin appears to be the glue that produces bonding. And the baby's distinctive look and behaviors cause oxytocin to be released in the fortunate adult. That appearance—the one that pulls an involuntary "aaah" out of us whenever we see a baby—and those oxytocin-inducing behaviors allow infants to recruit adults to be their nurturers, essential if such vulnerable and incompletely developed creatures are to survive.

The power of neoteny to recruit protectors and nurturers was vividly illustrated in the former Soviet Union. Forty years ago, a Soviet scientist decided to start breeding silver foxes for neoteny at a Siberian fur farm. The goal was to create a tamer fox that would go with less fuss to slaughter than the typical silver fox. Only the least aggressive, most approachable animals were bred.

The experiment continued for 40 years, and today, after 35 generations, the farm is home to a breed of tame foxes that look and act more like juvenile foxes and even dogs than like their wild forebears. The physical changes in the animals are remarkable (some have floppy, dog-like ears), but what is truly stunning is the change neoteny has wrought in the human response to them. Instead of taking advantage of the fact that these neotenic animals don't snap and snarl on the way to their deaths, their human keepers appear to have been recruited by their newly cute and endearing charges. The keepers and the foxes appear to have formed close bonds, so close that the keepers are trying to find ways to save the animals from slaughter.

1949 Rittenberg was initially jailed, without explanation, by former friends in Chairman Mao Zedong's government and spent his first year in total darkness when he wasn't being interrogated. (Rittenberg later learned that his arrest came at the behest of Communist Party officials in Moscow, who had wrongly identified him as a CIA agent.) Thrown into jail, confined to a tiny, pitch-dark cell, Rittenberg did not rail or panic. Instead, within minutes, he remembered a stanza of verse, four lines recited to him when he was a small child:

They drew a circle that shut me out,
Heretic, rebel, a thing to flout.
But love and I had the wit to win,
We drew a circle that took them in!

That bit of verse (adapted from "Outwitted," a poem by Edwin Markham) was the key to Rittenberg's survival. "My God," he thought, "there's my strategy." He drew the prison guards into his circle, developing relationships that would help him adapt to his confinement. Fluent in Chinese, he persuaded the guards to deliver him books and, eventually, provide a candle so that he could read. He also decided, after his first year, to devote himself to improving his mind—making it more scientific, more pure, and more dedicated to socialism. He believed that if he raised his consciousness, his captors would understand him better. And when, over time, the years in the dark began to take an intellectual toll on him and he found his reason faltering, he could still summon fairy tales and childhood stories such as *The Little Engine That Could* and take comfort from their simple messages.

By contrast, many of Rittenberg's fellow prisoners either lashed out in anger or withdrew. "They tended to go up the wall . . . They couldn't make it. And I think the reason was that they didn't understand . . . that happiness . . . is not a function of your circumstances; it's a function of your outlook on life."

Rittenberg's commitment to his ideals continued upon his release. His cell door opened suddenly in 1955, after his first six-year term in prison. He recounts, "Here was a representative of the central government telling me that I had been wronged, that the government was making a formal apology to me . . . and that they would do everything possible to make restitution." When his captors offered him money to start a new life in the United States or to travel in Europe, Rittenberg declined, choosing instead to stay in China and continue his work for the Communist Party.

And even after a second arrest, which put him into solitary confinement for ten years as retaliation for his support of open democracy during the Cultural Revolution, Rittenberg did not allow his spirit to be broken. Instead, he used his time in prison as an opportunity to question his belief system—in particular, his commitment to Marxism and Chairman Mao. "In that sense, prison emancipated me," he says.

Rittenberg studied, read, wrote, and thought, and he learned something about himself in the process: "I realized I had this great fear of being a turncoat, which . . . was so powerful that it prevented me from even looking at [my assumptions] . . . Even to question was an act of betrayal. After I got out . . . the scales fell away from my eyes and I understood that . . . the basic doctrine of arriving at democracy through dictatorship was wrong."

What's more, Rittenberg emerged from prison certain that absolutely nothing in his professional life could break him and went on to start a company with his wife. Rittenberg Associates is a consulting firm dedicated to developing business ties between the United States and China. Today, Rittenberg is as committed to his ideals—if not to his view of the best way to get there—as he was 50 years ago, when he was so severely tested.

Meeting Great Expectations

Fortunately, not all crucible experiences are traumatic. In fact, they can involve a positive, if deeply challenging, experience such as having a demanding boss or mentor. Judge Nathaniel R. Jones of the U.S. Court of Appeals for the Sixth Circuit, for instance, attributes much of his success to his interaction with a splendid mentor. That mentor was J. Maynard Dickerson, a successful attorney—the first black city prosecutor in the United States—and editor of a local African-American newspaper.

Dickerson influenced Jones at many levels. For instance, the older man brought Jones behind the scenes to witness firsthand the great civil rights struggle of the 1950s, inviting him to sit in on conversations with activists like Thurgood Marshall, Walter White, Roy Wilkins, and Robert C. Weaver. Says Jones, "I was struck by their resolve, their humor . . . and their determination not to let the system define them. Rather than just feel beaten down, they turned it around." The experience no doubt influenced the many important opinions Judge Jones has written in regard to civil rights.

Dickerson was both model and coach. His lessons covered every aspect of Jones's intellectual growth and presentation of self, including schooling in what we now call "emotional intelligence." Dickerson set the highest standards for Jones, especially in the area of communication skills—a facility we've found essential to leadership. Dickerson edited Jones's early attempts at writing a sports column with respectful ruthlessness, in red ink, as Jones remembers to this day—marking up the copy so that it looked, as Jones says, "like something chickens had a fight over." But Dickerson also took the time to explain every single mistake and why it mattered.

His mentor also expected the teenage Jones to speak correctly at all times and would hiss discreetly in his direction if he stumbled. Great expectations are evidence of great respect, and as Jones learned all the complex, often subtle lessons of how to succeed, he was motivated in no small measure by his desire not to disappoint the man he still calls "Mr. Dickerson." Dickerson gave Jones the kind of intensive mentoring that was tantamount to grooming him for a kind of professional and moral succession—and Jones has indeed become an instrument for the profound societal change for which Dickerson fought so courageously as well. Jones found life-changing meaning in the attention Dickerson paid to him—attention fueled by a conviction that he, too, though only a teenager, had a vital role to play in society and an important destiny.

Another story of a powerful mentor came to us from Michael Klein, a young man who made millions in Southern California real estate while still in his teens, only to lose it by the time he turned 20 and then go on to start several other businesses. His mentor was his grandfather Max S. Klein, who created the paint-by-numbers fad that swept the United States in the 1950s and 1960s. Klein was only four or five years old when his grandfather approached him and offered to share his business expertise. Over the years, Michael Klein's grandfather taught him to learn from and to cope with change, and the two spoke by phone for an hour every day until shortly before Max Klein's death.

The Essentials of Leadership

In our interviews, we heard many other stories of crucible experiences. Take Jack Coleman, 78-year-old former president of Haverford College in Pennsylvania. He told us of one day, during the Vietnam War, when he heard that a group of students was planning to pull down the American flag and burn it—and that former members of the school's football team were going to make sure the students didn't succeed. Seemingly out of nowhere, Coleman had the idea to preempt the violence by suggesting that the protesting students take down the flag, wash it, and then put it back up—a crucible moment that even now elicits tremendous emotion in Coleman as he describes that day.

There's also Common Cause founder John W. Gardner, who died earlier this year at 89. He identified his arduous training as a Marine during World War II as the crucible in which his leadership abilities emerged. Architect Frank Gehry spoke of the biases he experienced as a Jew in college. Jeff Wilke, a general manager at a major manufacturer, told us of the day he learned that an employee had been killed in his plant—an experience that taught him that leadership was about much more than making quarterly numbers.

So, what allowed these people to not only cope with these difficult situations but also learn from them? We believe that great leaders possess four essential skills, and, we were surprised to learn, these happen to be the same skills that allow a person to find meaning in what could be a debilitating experience. First is the ability to engage others in shared meaning. Consider Sidney Harman, who dived into a chaotic work environment to mobilize employees around an entirely new approach to management. Second is a distinctive and compelling voice. Look at Jack Coleman's ability to defuse a potentially violent situation with only his words. Third is a sense of integrity (including a strong set of values). Here, we point again to Coleman, whose values prevailed even during the emotionally charged clash between peace demonstrators and the angry (and strong) former football team members.

But by far the most critical skill of the four is what we call "adaptive capacity." This is, in essence, applied creativity—an almost magical ability to transcend adversity, with all its attendant stresses, and to emerge stronger than before. It's composed of two primary qualities: the ability to grasp context, and hardiness. The ability to grasp context implies an ability to weigh a welter of factors, ranging from how very different groups of people will interpret a gesture to being able to put a situation in perspective. Without this, leaders are utterly lost, because they cannot connect with their constituents. M. Douglas Ivester, who succeeded Roberto Goizueta at Coca-Cola, exhibited a woeful inability to grasp context, lasting just 28 months on the job. For example, he demoted his highest-ranked African-American employee even as the company was losing a $200 million class-action suit brought by black employees—and this in Atlanta, a city with a powerful African-American majority. Contrast Ivester with Vernon Jordan. Jordan realized his boss's time was up—not just his time in power, but the era that formed him. And so Jordan was able to see past the insults and recognize his boss's bitterness for what it was—desperate lashing out.

Hardiness is just what it sounds like—the perseverance and toughness that enable people to emerge from devastating circumstances without losing hope. Look at Michael Klein, who experienced failure but didn't let it defeat him. He found himself with a single asset—a tiny software company he'd acquired. Klein built it into Transoft Networks, which Hewlett-Packard acquired in 1999. Consider, too, Mickie Siebert, who used her sense of humor to curtail offensive conversations. Or Sidney Rittenberg's strength during his imprisonment. He drew on his personal memories and inner strength to emerge from his lengthy prison term without bitterness.

It is the combination of hardiness and ability to grasp context that, above all, allows a person to not only survive an ordeal, but to learn from it, and to emerge stronger, more engaged, and more committed than ever. These attributes allow leaders to grow from their crucibles, instead of being destroyed by them—to find opportunity where others might find only despair. This is the stuff of true leadership.

Originally published in September 2002. Reprint R0209B

Building Resilience

by Martin E.P. Seligman

DOUGLAS AND WALTER, two University of Pennsylvania MBA graduates, were laid off by their Wall Street companies 18 months ago. Both went into a tailspin: They were sad, listless, indecisive, and anxious about the future. For Douglas, the mood was transient. After two weeks he told himself, "It's not you; it's the economy going through a bad patch. I'm good at what I do, and there will be a market for my skills." He updated his résumé and sent it to a dozen New York firms, all of which rejected him. He then tried six companies in his Ohio hometown and eventually landed a position. Walter, by contrast, spiraled into hopelessness: "I got fired because I can't perform under pressure," he thought. "I'm not cut out for finance. The economy will take years to recover." Even as the market improved, he didn't look for another job; he ended up moving back in with his parents.

Douglas and Walter (actually composites based on interviewees) stand at opposite ends of the continuum of reactions to failure. The Douglases of the world bounce back after a brief period of malaise; within a year they've grown because of the experience. The Walters go from sadness to depression to a paralyzing fear of the future. Yet failure is a nearly inevitable part of work; and along with dashed romance, it is one of life's most common traumas. People like Walter are almost certain to find their careers stymied, and companies full of such employees are doomed in hard times. It is people like Douglas who rise to the top, and whom organizations must recruit and retain in order to succeed. But how can you tell who is a Walter and who is a Douglas? And can Walters become Douglases? Can resilience be measured and taught?

Thirty years of scientific research has put the answers to these questions within our reach. We have learned not only how to distinguish those who will grow after failure from those who will collapse, but also how to build the skills of people in the latter category. I have worked with colleagues from around the world to develop a program for teaching resilience. It is now being tested in an organization of 1.1 million people where trauma is more common and more severe than in any corporate setting: the U.S. Army. Its members may struggle with depression and post-traumatic stress disorder (PTSD), but thousands of them also experience post-traumatic growth. Our goal is to employ resilience training to reduce the number of those who struggle and increase the number of those who grow. We believe that businesspeople can draw lessons from this approach, particularly in times of failure and stagnation. Working with both individual soldiers (employees) and drill sergeants (managers), we are helping to create an army of Douglases who can turn their most difficult experiences into catalysts for improved performance.

Optimism Is the Key

Although I'm now called the father of positive psychology, I came to it the long, hard way, through many years of research on failure and helplessness. In the late 1960s I was part of the team that discovered "learned helplessness." We found that dogs, rats, mice, and even cockroaches that experienced mildly painful shock over which they had no control would eventually just accept it, with no attempt to escape. It was next shown that human beings do the same thing. In an experiment published in 1975 by Donald Hiroto and me and replicated many times since, subjects are randomly divided into three groups. Those in the first are exposed to an annoying loud noise that they can stop by pushing a button in front of them. Those in the second hear the same noise but can't turn it off, though they try hard. Those in the third, the control group, hear nothing at all. Later, typi-

Idea in Brief

Failure is one of life's most common traumas, yet people's responses to it vary widely. Some bounce back after a brief period of malaise; others descend into depression and a paralyzing fear of the future.

Thirty years of research suggests that resilience can be measured and taught—and the U.S. Army is putting that idea to the test with a program called Comprehensive Soldier Fitness. The aim of CSF is to make soldiers as fit psychologically as they are physically.

A key component of CSF is "master resilience training" for drill sergeants—a form of management training that teaches leaders how to embrace resilience and then pass it on, by building mental toughness, signature strengths, and strong relationships.

cally the following day, the subjects are faced with a brand-new situation that again involves noise. To turn the noise off, all they have to do is move their hands about 12 inches. The people in the first and third groups figure this out and readily learn to avoid the noise. But those in the second group typically do nothing. In phase one they failed, realized they had no control, and became passive. In phase two, expecting more failure, they don't even try to escape. They have learned helplessness.

Strangely, however, about a third of the animals and people who experience inescapable shocks or noise never become helpless. What is it about them that makes this so? Over 15 years of study, my colleagues and I discovered that the answer is optimism. We developed questionnaires and analyzed the content of verbatim speech and writing to assess "explanatory style" as optimistic or pessimistic. We discovered that people who don't give up have a habit of interpreting setbacks as temporary, local, and changeable. ("It's going away quickly; it's just this one situation, and I can do something about it.") That suggested how we might immunize people against learned helplessness, against depression and anxiety, and against giving up after failure: by teaching them to think like optimists. We created the Penn Resiliency Program, under the direction of Karen Reivich and Jane Gillham, of the University of Pennsylvania, for young adults and children. The program has been replicated in 21

What Are Your Strengths?

THE VALUES IN ACTION signature strengths survey measures 24 positive character traits, among them curiosity, creativity, bravery, persistence, integrity, fairness, leadership, and self-regulation. Participants rank statements on a scale from "very much like me" to "very much unlike me" to determine the areas in which they shine. Here is a sampling:

- I find the world a very interesting place.
- I always identify the reasons for my actions.
- I never quit a task before it is done.
- Being able to come up with new and different ideas is one of my strong points.
- I have taken frequent stands in the face of strong opposition.
- I am always willing to take risks to establish a relationship.
- I always admit when I am wrong.
- In a group, I try to make sure everyone feels included.
- I always look on the bright side.
- I want to fully participate in life, not just view it from the sidelines.

diverse school settings—ranging from suburbs to inner cities, from Philadelphia to Beijing. We also created a 10-day program in which teachers learn techniques for becoming more optimistic in their own lives and how to teach those techniques to their students. We've found that it reduces depression and anxiety in the children under their care. (Another way we teach positive psychology is through the master of applied positive psychology, or MAPP, degree program, now in its sixth year at Penn.)

In November 2008, when the legendary General George W. Casey, Jr., the army chief of staff and former commander of the multinational force in Iraq, asked me what positive psychology had to say about soldiers' problems, I offered a simple answer: How human beings react to extreme adversity is normally distributed. On one end are the people who fall apart into PTSD, depression, and even suicide. In the middle are most people, who at first react with symptoms of depression and anxiety but within a month or so are, by physical and psychological measures, back where they were before the trauma. That is resilience. On the other end are people who show post-traumatic growth. They, too, first experience depression and anxiety, often exhibiting full-blown PTSD, but within a year they are better off than they were before the trauma. These are the people of whom Friedrich Nietzsche said, "That which does not kill us makes us stronger."

I told General Casey that the army could shift its distribution toward the growth end by teaching psychological skills to stop the downward spiral that often follows failure. He ordered the organization to measure resilience and teach positive psychology to create a force as fit psychologically as it is physically. This $145 million initiative, under the direction of Brigadier General Rhonda Cornum, is called Comprehensive Soldier Fitness (CSF) and consists of three components: a test for psychological fitness, self-improvement courses available following the test, and "master resilience training" (MRT) for drill sergeants. These are based on PERMA: positive emotion, engagement, relationships, meaning, and accomplishment—the building blocks of resilience and growth.

Testing for Psychological Fitness

A team led by the University of Michigan professor Christopher Peterson, author of the Values in Action signature strengths survey, created the test, called the Global Assessment Tool (GAT). It is a 20-minute questionnaire that focuses on strengths rather than weaknesses and is designed to measure four things: emotional, family, social, and spiritual fitness. All four have been credited with reducing depression and anxiety. According to research, they are the keys to PERMA.

Although individual scores are confidential, the GAT results allow test takers to choose appropriate basic or advanced courses for building resilience. The GAT also provides a common vocabulary for describing soldiers' assets. The data generated will allow the army to gauge the psychosocial fitness both of particular units and of the entire organization, highlighting positives and negatives. At this writing, more than 900,000 soldiers have taken the test. The army will compare psychological profiles with performance and medical results over time; the resulting database will enable us to answer questions like these: What specific strengths protect against PTSD, depression, anxiety, and suicide? Does a strong sense of meaning result in better performance? Are people who score high in positive emotion promoted more quickly? Can optimism spread from a leader to his troops?

Online Courses

The second component of CSF is optional online courses in each of the four fitnesses and one mandatory course on post-traumatic growth. The implications for corporate managers are more obvious for some modules than for others, but I'll briefly explain them all.

The emotional fitness module, created by Barbara Fredrickson, a professor of emotions and psychophysiology at the University of North Carolina, and her colleague Sara Algoe, teaches soldiers how to amplify positive emotions and how to recognize when negative ones, such as sadness and anger, are out of proportion to the reality of the threat they face.

Family fitness, too, affects work performance, and cell phones, e-mail, Facebook, and Skype allow even soldiers on combat duty, or expats on assignment, to remain intimately involved with their families. A course created by John and Julie Gottman, eminent psychologists specializing in marriage, focuses on building a variety of relationship skills—including fostering trust, constructively managing conflict, creating shared meaning, and recovering from betrayal.

The social fitness module, developed by John Cacioppo, a professor of psychology at the University of Chicago and an expert on loneliness, teaches empathy to soldiers by explaining mirror neurons in the brain. When you see another person in pain, your brain activity is similar but not identical to what it is when you yourself are in pain. The module then asks soldiers to practice identifying emotions in others, with an emphasis on racial and cultural diversity. This is at the heart of developing emotional intelligence—and diversity in the U.S. Army is a way of life, not just a political slogan.

The spiritual fitness module, created by Kenneth Pargament, a professor of psychology at Bowling Green State University, and Colonel Patrick Sweeney, a professor of behavioral sciences and leadership at West Point, takes soldiers through the process of building a "spiritual core" with self-awareness, a sense of agency, self-regulation, self-motivation, and social awareness. "Spiritual" in CSF refers not to religion but to belonging to and serving something larger than the self.

The mandatory module, on post-traumatic growth, is highly relevant for business executives facing failure. Created by Richard Tedeschi, a professor of psychology at the University of North Carolina at Charlotte, and the Harvard psychologist Richard McNally, it begins with the ancient wisdom that personal transformation comes from a renewed appreciation of being alive, enhanced personal strength, acting on new possibilities, improved relationships, or spiritual deepening. The module interactively teaches soldiers about five elements known to contribute to post-traumatic growth:

1. Understanding the response to trauma (read "failure"), which includes shattered beliefs about the self, others, and the future. This is a normal response, not a symptom of PTSD or a character defect.

2. Reducing anxiety through techniques for controlling intrusive thoughts and images.

3. Engaging in constructive self-disclosure. Bottling up trauma can lead to a worsening of physical and psychological symptoms, so soldiers are encouraged to tell their stories.

4. Creating a narrative in which the trauma is seen as a fork in the road that enhances the appreciation of paradox—loss and gain, grief and gratitude, vulnerability and strength. A manager might compare this to what the leadership studies pioneer Warren Bennis called "crucibles of leadership." The narrative specifies what personal strengths were called upon, how some

relationships improved, how spiritual life strengthened, how life itself was better appreciated, or what new doors opened.

5. Articulating life principles. These encompass new ways to be altruistic, crafting a new identity, and taking seriously the idea of the Greek hero who returns from Hades to tell the world an important truth about how to live.

Master Resilience Training

The third and most important component of Comprehensive Soldier Fitness is the master resilience training for drill sergeants and other leaders, given at the University of Pennsylvania; at Victory University, in Memphis, Tennessee; at Fort Jackson, South Carolina; and by mobile teams working with troops in Germany and Korea. MRT can be seen as management training—teaching leaders how to embrace resilience and then pass on the knowledge. The content of MRT divides into three parts—building mental toughness, building signature strengths, and building strong relationships. All three are patterned after the Penn Resiliency Program and use plenary lectures, breakout sessions that include role playing, work sheets, and small-group discussion.

Building mental toughness

This segment of MRT is similar in theme to the online emotional fitness course for individual soldiers. It starts with Albert Ellis's ABCD model: C (emotional consequences) stem not directly from A (adversity) but from B (one's beliefs about adversity). The sergeants work through a series of A's (falling out of a three-mile run, for example) and learn to separate B's—heat-of-the-moment thoughts about the situation ("I'm a failure")—from C's, the emotions generated by those thoughts (such as feeling down for the rest of the day and thus performing poorly in the next training exercise). They then learn D—how to quickly and effectively dispel unrealistic beliefs about adversity.

Next we focus on thinking traps, such as overgeneralizing or judging a person's worth or ability on the basis of a single action. We illustrate this as follows: "A soldier in your unit struggles to keep up during physical training and is dragging the rest of the day. His uniform looks sloppy, and he makes a couple of mistakes during artillery practice. It might be natural to think that he lacks the stuff of a soldier. But what effect does that have on both the thinker and the other soldier?" We also discuss "icebergs"—deeply held beliefs such as "Asking for help is a sign of weakness"—and teach a technique for identifying and eliminating those that cause out-of-kilter emotional reactions: Does the iceberg remain meaningful? Is it accurate in the given situation? Is it overly rigid? Is it useful?

Finally, we deal with how to minimize catastrophic thinking by considering worst-case, best-case, and most likely outcomes. For example, a sergeant receives a negative performance evaluation from his commanding officer. He thinks, "I won't be recommended for promotion, and I don't have what it takes to stay in the army." That's the worst case. Now let's put it in perspective. What's the best case? "The negative report was a mistake." And what's the most likely case? "I will receive a corrective action plan from my counselor, and I will follow it. I'll be frustrated, and my squad leader will be disappointed."

Building signature strengths

The second part of the training begins with a test similar to the GAT—Peterson's Values in Action signature strengths survey, which is taken online and produces a ranked list of the test taker's top 24 character strengths. (See the sidebar "What Are Your Strengths?") Small groups discuss these questions: What did you learn about yourself from the survey? Which strengths have you developed through your military service? How do your strengths contribute to your completing a mission and reaching your goals? What are the shadow sides of your strengths, and how can you minimize them? Then the sergeants are put on teams and told to tackle a mission using the team members' character-strength profiles. Finally, the sergeants write their own "strengths in challenges" stories. One sergeant described how he used his strengths of love, wisdom, and gratitude to help a soldier who was acting out and stirring up conflict. The sergeant discovered that the soldier felt consumed by anger at his wife, and the anger spilled over to his unit. The sergeant used his wisdom to help the soldier understand the wife's perspective and worked with him to write a letter in which the soldier described the gratitude he felt because his wife had handled so much on her own during his three deployments.

Building strong relationships

The third part of MRT focuses on practical tools for positive communication. We draw on the work of Shelly Gable, a psychology professor at UC Santa Barbara, which shows that when an individual responds actively and constructively (as opposed to passively and destructively) to someone who is sharing a positive experience, love and friendship increase. (See the sidebar "Four Ways to Respond.") The sergeants complete a work sheet about how they typically respond and identify factors that may get in the way of active and constructive responses (such as being tired or overly focused on themselves). Next we teach the work of the Stanford psychology professor Carol Dweck on effective praise. When, for example, a sergeant mentions specifics (as opposed to saying something general like "Good job!"), his soldiers know that their leader was paying attention and that the praise is authentic. We also teach assertive communication, distinguishing it from passive or aggressive communication. What is the language, voice tone, body language, and pace of each of the three styles, and what messages do they convey?

Enhancing mental toughness, highlighting and honing strengths, and fostering strong relationships are core competencies for any successful manager. Leadership development programs often touch on these skills, but the MRT program brings them together in systematic form to ensure that even in the face of terrible failures—those that cost lives—army sergeants know how to help the men and women under their command flourish rather than flounder. Managers can change the culture of their organizations to focus on the positive

Four Ways To Respond

IN MASTER RESILIENCE TRAINING we explain and demonstrate the four styles of responding: *active constructive* (authentic, enthusiastic support), *passive constructive* (laconic support), *passive destructive* (ignoring the event), and *active destructive* (pointing out negative aspects of the event).

Here's an example: Private Johnson tells Private Gonzales, "Hey, I just got a promotion."

Active constructive

"That's great. What are your new duties? When do you start? What did the captain say about why you deserved it?"

Passive constructive

"That's nice."

Passive destructive

"I got a funny e-mail from my son. Listen to this…"

Active destructive

"You know there's no extra pay, and it will eat up a lot of your R&R time."

---

instead of the negative and, in doing so, turn pessimistic, helpless Walters into optimistic, can-do Douglases. Frankly, we were nervous that these hard-boiled soldiers would find resilience training "girly" or "touchy-feely" or "psychobabble." They did not; in fact, they gave the course an average rating of 4.9 out of 5.0. A large number of them say it's the best course they've ever had in the army.

We believe that MRT will build a better army. Our hypothesis is being tested in a large-scale study under the command of Lieutenant Colonel Sharon McBride and Captain Paul Lester. As the program rolls out, they are comparing the performance of soldiers who have been taught resilience by their sergeants with that of soldiers who haven't. When they are finished, we will know conclusively whether resilience training and positive psychology can make adults in a large organization more effective, as they have done for younger people in schools.

Originally published in April 2011. Reprint R1104H

Cognitive Fitness

by Roderick Gilkey and Clint Kilts

WINSTON CHURCHILL WAS OUTSPOKEN on the sacred rites of smoking cigars and drinking alcohol before, after, and during meals—and in the intervals in between. But he was also exceptionally active mentally. As historians have duly noted, Churchill went on to live until 90. That speaks volumes for the information that is now coming to light about how the brain can affect the body.

Of course, few executives would be willing to follow Churchill's example in taking such poor care of their physical health. As life expectancy continues to rise, people are doing more and more to ensure that their lives, if long, are going to be healthy. The American Heart Association now recommends 30 minutes of moderate exercise five days a week. Not surprisingly, most large companies offer health club memberships as a perk; many provide gyms on-site. Find yourself on the road, and you're almost guaranteed to have a fitness center in your hotel. You may even have to get in line to use the equipment.

Until recently, however, there seemed to be no guidelines for active efforts you could make to stay *mentally* healthy. There were no brain exercises—no mental push-ups—you could do to stave off the loss of memory and analytic acuity that comes as you grow older. In the worst-case scenario, you could end up with Alzheimer's disease, for which there are no proven treatments.

But a concentrated commitment of resources by the National Institutes of Health, the National Institute of Mental Health, and the Library of Congress during the 1990s—which the White House proclaimed the "decade of the brain" to heighten public awareness of the need for neuroscience research—yielded a broad front of research and training that has upended some deeply held beliefs about the brain. One such belief is that the brain necessarily diminishes with age. It turns out that neurons, the basic cells that allow information transfer to support the brain's computing power, do *not* have to die off as we get older. In fact, a number of regions of the brain important to functions such as motor behavior and memory can actually expand their complement of neurons as we age. This process, called neurogenesis, used to be unthinkable in mainstream neuroscience.

What does all this have to do with you? The process of neurogenesis is profoundly affected by the way you live your life. The brain's anatomy, neural networks, and cognitive abilities can all be strengthened and improved through your experiences and interactions with your environment. The health of your brain isn't just the product of negative and positive childhood experiences and genetic inheritance; it reflects your adult choices and experiences as well. That's extremely good news. Sigmund Freud and those who followed him both in the neurological sciences and in the psychoanalytic tradition thought for years that brain development ceased in childhood or early adolescence. Although these periods do hold the greatest potential for neural development, we now know there is a regimen you can follow to retain and even build mental capacity as you age.

Brain-imaging studies indicate, for example, that acquired expertise in areas as diverse as playing a cello, juggling, speaking a foreign language, and driving a taxicab expands and makes more communicative the neural systems in the parts of the brain responsible for motor control and spatial navigation. In other words, you can make physical changes in your brain by learning new skills. You can even make changes in how your brain functions by exercising conscious will. In a recent experiment using real-time brain imaging, scientists demonstrated that individuals learned to mitigate the sensation of pain by consciously controlling the observable activity of the rostral anterior cingulate cortex, an area of the brain involved in pain processing. In theory, therefore, it's possible for people to alleviate pain through neurofeedback, without drugs.

These advances in neuroscience suggest that there is no reason why your brain at 60 can't be as competent as it was at 25. That would not have been news to thinkers such as Socrates, Copernicus, and Galileo, who were all still at the peak of their intellectual powers in their sixties and seventies. Nor would it surprise business leaders such as Alan Greenspan, Warren Buffett, and Sumner Redstone. These icons and others like them have intuitively understood that the brain's alertness is the result of what we call cognitive fitness— a state of optimized ability to reason, remember, learn, plan, and adapt that is enhanced by certain attitudes, lifestyle choices, and exercises. The more cognitively fit you are, the better you will be able to make decisions, solve problems, and deal with stress and change. Cognitive fitness will allow you to be more open to new ideas and alternative perspectives. It will give you the capacity to change your behaviors and forecast their outcomes in order to realize your goals. You can become the kind of person your company values most. Perhaps more important, you can delay senescence for years and even enjoy a second career.

So how can you become cognitively fit? Drawing selectively from the rapidly expanding body of neuroscience research as well as from well-established research in psychology and other mental health fields, we have identified four steps you can take. These steps are by no means exhaustive. They overlap and reinforce one another. Together they capture, we believe, some of the key opportunities for maintaining an engaged, creative brain.

Step 1: Understand How Experience Makes the Brain Grow

The experience-dependent nature of cognitive health has long been appreciated by psychologists. As early as the middle of the twentieth century, they noted that rich experience helped very young children to interact with their environment. We've also known for some time that experience has a physiological impact on the brain. In the late eighteenth century, the Italian anatomist Vincenzo Malacarne conducted a famous series of controlled experiments on dogs and birds. He separated each litter or set of eggs into pairs, giving extensive care and training over time to one animal from every pair, and good care but no training to the other. His later autopsies revealed that the trained animals' brains were more anatomically complex, with more folds and fissures. This research was the first to identify the impact of experience and education on the structure of the brain. To build on an example mentioned earlier, the expansion of the motor area representing a hand that plays a cello is greater in someone who started lessons early in life than in someone who didn't.

While the neuroscience community has known for quite a while about the biological impact of expanding experience, we've only recently figured out how the brain actually processes experience in order to encode learning and build performance capacity. The discovery of dedicated neural systems that represent objects, people, and actions provides a new explanation of the mechanism involved. The so-called mirror neurons making up these systems aid the speed and accuracy of our perception by mentally simulating objects and actions in our environment. Knowing that mirror neurons allow us to internally reflect our external world is a quantum leap in our understanding of how humans comprehend and master their environment. Experience gained through observation activates these performance-enhancing neurons, which accelerate learning and the capacity to learn.

Traditionally, scientists have assumed that people gain new skills through practice—that is, through direct experience—but the existence of mirror neurons means you can also gain skills through observation and indirect experience. Think about this for a moment: When a golf pro demonstrates the correct stance and swing for you to imitate, mirror neurons are activated, enabling you to learn from his experience by supplying you with the mental image of the correct actions. And it's not just physical skills that can be picked up this way. Your social cognitions are similarly aided by specialized neurons that reflect facial expressions, gestures, and other signals, and develop your ability to read other people's actions and expressions by matching them with internal representations you have acquired.

This suggests that mental imagery—for instance, trying to re-create the golf pro's swing through a mental picture—is a valid mode of learning and acquiring new competences. Indeed, sports professionals often attribute their exceptional abilities to being able to "see" the ball and its flight prior to striking or catching it. The brain's ability to learn in this way makes a biological case for the use of simulations and case studies as tools in your quest for development as a leader. Such approaches not only promise effective ways of learning but are also potentially very efficient. You can conceivably gain the brain benefits of other people's long-term direct experience through, for example, short-term exposure to simulation. Simulated experiences can establish neural readiness for real experiences.

Of course, direct experience remains the keystone of a person's brain development—but we increasingly understand how to pave the way for such experience. One of the most powerful tools available for strengthening the executive brain is the walkabout. In business, this is known as management by walking around—the practice of getting out of your office and talking to employees. It's not just good business practice; it is also a sound form of cognitive exercise.

The walkabout is named after an Australian rite of passage in which aboriginal adolescents undertake a prolonged and challenging physical journey, sometimes for several months, in search of psychological and spiritual self-definition and maturity. The timing is just right, since it is during adolescence that the brain establishes and integrates the neural networks in the prefrontal cortex that encode a sense of self-identity, as well as moral and social conduct. This process culminates in late adolescence, when the brain's neurons are fully myelinated (coated with insulation) and interconnected in networks that help the mature brain function in an efficient, organized manner. The walkabout is not, of course, the only rite-of-passage ritual; it's quite remarkable how many similar rituals occur in different cultures at precisely the same stage in people's lives. There is a generally accepted understanding that adolescents need such "peak" experiences to consolidate their personal histories and their physical development into a viable, more advanced identity.

This sort of journey, more broadly speaking, can also have a strong influence on an executive's career, particularly if the timing is right. Warren Buffett is one leader who realizes this. When Anne Mulcahy, the CEO of Xerox, sought his advice about how to help the company emerge from a financial crisis that was rapidly pushing it toward bankruptcy, he urged her to engage in a walkabout. His advice was that she should learn what Xerox employees and customers were thinking and worry less about what the financial analysts and shareholders were saying. It made excellent sense from a neurological standpoint for Mulcahy to acquire at the beginning of her tenure as CEO a deeper understanding of the people who would be following her, because the neural networks that would enable her decision making as a leader would not yet be fully formed. If she had stayed isolated in the corner office, those networks would certainly have ended up looking different than they do today.

Step 2: Work Hard at Play

Another one of the most effective ways you can promote your cognitive health is to engage in the serious business of play. As the philosopher Henri Bergson wrote, "To exist is to change, to change is to mature, to mature is to go on creating oneself endlessly." To do this well requires consciously drawing on one of the great legacies of childhood—our ability to play, which lies at the heart of our capacity to imagine and invent.

The origin of the word "play" is telling: It is derived from the Old English word "plegian," which means to exercise. As a verb, "play" is often defined in terms of individual or group imaginative activity that promotes discovery and learning, or social activity that promotes what psychologist Daniel Goleman would call emotional and social intelligence. As a noun, it refers to activity engaged in for enjoyment or recreation. In both senses, it is closely tied to pleasure and strongly associated with the brain's reward systems. Indeed, Jaak Panksepp's neuroscientific research on mammals identified play as a primary human drive and the brain's source of joy, which is linked to the release of a specific neurochemical that modulates gene expression critical to the development of a child's social brain. Joy provides what has been described as "emotional fuel," which helps the brain develop and expand its synaptic networks. In early life, this neurochemical appears in lower subcortical regions, which later, according to Panksepp and his colleagues, contribute to the growth and development of higher brain functions associated with the frontal cortex. So play is not only a psychological precursor of social and emotional maturity in adulthood; it is a physiological one as well.

As you go about the hard work of your career, it is critical to remember to play. That's because in adult life, play engages the prefrontal cortex (our most highly evolved and recently acquired brain areas), nourishing our highest-level cognitive functions—those related to incentive and reward processing, goal and skill representation, mental imagery, self-knowledge, and memory, just to name a few. Play, therefore, improves your ability to reason and understand the world. Our most brilliant thinkers and leaders know this. Albert Einstein, for example, saw his ability to grasp profound insights into the nature of the universe as a result of combinatory play. When asked to describe his experience in developing the theory of relativity, he observed that it began as a "physical sensation" that later became a set of visual images and finally emerged as a written formula that he could begin to describe in words and symbols. This sounds less like an adult's process of analytical reasoning than like a child's creation of a fantasy world, where characters magically pop into being, which no doubt is why Einstein concluded that "imagination is more important than knowledge."

Play is a tool that we must consciously use, as the demands on us increasingly call for greater levels of emotional control—but as we get older, we unfortunately tend to play less often. Here's how Daniel Goleman describes the process: "As a child matures, the circuitry for emotional control will slowly suppress the effervescent urge to giggle and romp. As the regulatory circuits of the prefrontal cortex develop in late childhood and the early teen years, children are more able to meet the social demands to 'get serious.'" The consequence is that play is relegated to the realm of distant memory, and its revitalizing capacities are reduced.

Some organizations go out of their way to let people experiment and play. A host of hard-driving Silicon Valley companies, such as Google and Apple, provide environments that encourage some kind of play, referred to variously as Zen dens, play spaces, and chat chambers. As the leaders of these companies realize, a legitimate and comfortable environment for brains to play can be a powerful tool for allowing people to develop their creative capacities and cognitive health. Conversely, in companies that stifle play, brainpower may actually decrease as it does in children with failure-to-thrive syndrome, a condition created by experientially deprived or abusive environments. One of the prototypical examples is ITT (particularly under former CEO Harold Geneen), which was once described in the *Wall Street Journal* as "a company that's continually going to disappoint you however low your expectations are."

A big challenge in finding the right environment for your brain to thrive is striking a balance between risk and security. You must have a stake in the game you play if you are to really engage in it; risk alerts the brain and activates capacities for both reason and imagination. If you don't allow for some risk in your career, you may become like an overprotected child who fails to explore the world with any autonomy and thus never fully achieves his potential. But too great a personal stake in the game creates stress, which activates the amygdala and other limbic brain areas that constitute the brain's homeland security system. When the limbic system kicks in, your brain reverts to instinctive, preprogrammed survival behaviors rather than engaging in higher-order learned ones. In extreme situations, stress can trigger anxiety disorders and chaotic behaviors. And the more driven you are, the greater the risk this will happen. Ambitious people don't like failing or looking stupid. As the social scientist Chris Argyris (one of the fathers of organizational-learning theory) put it, smart people have trouble learning because it involves so much floundering and failure. Play is hard work.

Step 3: Search for Patterns

As most people know, the brain is composed of two hemispheres that have interconnected but very different functions. Neuroscience technology and research have provided us with a more complete picture of the left and right hemispheres' specialized roles. The left hemisphere is the primary source of neural information that a person uses to carry out routine tasks. The right deals with novelty, including experience and data that are less linear and less structured linguistically or mathematically. The right hemisphere is the more "poetic" part of the brain; it operates in metaphorical, image-based, imaginative ways. In this section of the article, we'll focus on what you as a leader can do to improve the functions of the left hemisphere, which often gets taken for granted as essentially determined by genetic inheritance.

Ironically, many cognitive fitness exercises directed at businesspeople focus on stimulating the right hemisphere—the creative, playful side. In part this is because of the classic stereotype of businesspeople as dull men in gray suits who need to loosen up. It's also true that in recent years creativity has come to be seen as the panacea for corporate ills. Although it's important to stimulate creative, divergent thinking, you'll derive just as much benefit, and perhaps more, from stimulating the analytic neural networks that are often viewed as left-hemispheric. These networks comprise the standard operating procedures that you use throughout a given day—a vast cognitive repository or library that is automatically activated to handle familiar tasks and challenges.

Why is the left hemisphere so important? Recent neuroimaging investigations have identified one of the engines that serve left-hemisphere performance: constellations of neurons that neuroscientists such as Elkhonon Goldberg call attractors, which mediate critical executive functions in the brain. While attractors are not exclusively located in the left hemisphere, they are especially supportive of the role played by that hemisphere. They are organized to orchestrate thought and action with great efficiency and effectiveness. Together they form the basis of what the Nobel laureate Herbert Simon referred to as pattern recognition, which he considered to be the most powerful cognitive tool we have at our disposal. Pattern recognition is the brain's ability to scan the environment; discern order and create meaning from huge amounts of data; and thereby quickly assess a situation so that appropriate action can be taken right away and with a high degree of accuracy. It is a complex chain reaction that uses the highest-level capacities for abstraction and reflection that are based on the deepest repositories of stored experience. The power of pattern recognition, a critical competence of the executive brain, can be seen in the capacity to simplify without being simplistic. For executives trying to make sense of a rapidly changing business environment, superiority in pattern recognition is perhaps the greatest competitive advantage that can be developed.

There's a lot that you can do to develop your left-hemispheric capabilities. First and foremost, challenge your existing mind-set, enlarge it, and make it more complex. Listen to different viewpoints, read new kinds of articles and books, and visit places with a focused set of learning objectives. All these experiences—particularly those related to your own organization or job—will expand your vocabulary, your conceptual storehouse, and your general perspective. Such immersions will call into question your own mind-set and improve your abilities in pattern recognition.

Hitachi Data Systems provides a good example of the kind of foray we're talking about. Working with BrightHouse, a consulting company based in Atlanta, Hitachi executives were invited to an ideation-strategy session with a distinguished classics professor to help them think about how to reposition their business. As a result of what they learned, some of the executives have been working on reorganizing the company along the lines of the Greek agora, with a view to creating an open marketplace for the exchange of ideas and knowledge. We're not saying that the classics professor told Hitachi what to do; rather, Hitachi's leaders combined what the classicist had to say about ancient Athens with what they knew about their company to create a new and potentially better way to share information.

With activities such as these, it is of utmost importance that you do them often. Make a consistent, ongoing commitment to immersing yourself in new systems and ways of thinking. It cannot be an occasional event, because the point is to expose yourself to a variety of cases and situations that cumulatively encode rich experience in your brain.

Just as you'll need to vary your own experiences to maximize your cognitive fitness, you'll also want to make sure that the experiences of your management team members are varied. Avoid filling the team with people who've all followed the same path upward. This advice may seem obvious, but we suggest taking a cold, hard look at how executives make it to the top in your organization. Isn't there a tendency for one route to dominate? This is natural, given that those who are looking for advancement tend to benchmark, and those at the top tend to warm to subordinates with experiences similar to their own. Evolutionary biology could give you any number of explanations for the survival value of these behaviors. But if you care about your company's cognitive fitness and, in particular, your management team's overall ability to discern patterns, then you need to be on guard against the inclination to pick only one kind of leader. Selection and succession programs that draw from the same limited population of executives promote an aggregation of cognitive templates based on shared experience and common pattern recognition. When a perspective becomes codified, people stop looking for new patterns and your company sacrifices some of its cognitive fitness—and competitiveness.

Step 4: Seek Novelty and Innovation

We have looked at the role of the left hemisphere in achieving the highest levels of cognitive fitness; now let's turn to the right hemisphere's contribution. The importance of expanding the brain's capacity to deal with novelty, a capacity typically associated with right-hemisphere functioning, becomes particularly obvious when we consider the fact that the right hemisphere deteriorates faster with age than the left.

The right hemisphere was once described by some neuroscientists as the "inferior" hemisphere in terms of cognitive functions, because it is the left side that governs our abilities in language and basic or linear logic. For many years, it wasn't clear how critical a role the right hemisphere played in obtaining the knowledge and wisdom that is later encoded in the left side. Research is now revealing that the right hemisphere is the exploratory part of the brain, dedicated to discovery and learning. When a child studies a language or an

Exercising Your Brain:
A Personal Program

BECAUSE THE BRAIN IS AN INTERACTIVE SYSTEM, any activities that stimulate one part of it can easily stimulate other parts. Therefore, our cognitive fitness categories need to be understood as approximations—this is particularly the case with hemispherically focused activity. Although some stimuli may initially create greater activations in, say, the right hemisphere, both hemispheres will ultimately be involved in the process of mastering new challenges. While there is much to learn about the intricacies of cognitive enhancement, we believe that the following exercises are a good selection.

Manage by walking about
Leave the executive dining room and drop by the company cafeteria, production floor, or loading docks. This could put you in unfamiliar territory, which is a good thing for broadening your perspective. What's more, the very act of walking and moving about invigorates your brain. That's why when you have a mental block on some problem you are solving, getting up and changing your environment can lead to an "aha" moment.

Read funny books
Humor promotes insight and enhances our health—even the immune system seems to love a good joke, as it is strengthened by the use of humor and the perspective it offers.

Play games
Activities like bridge, chess, sudoku, and the *New York Times* crossword puzzle all provide good neural workouts. There are ever more possibilities online, too, with the growing popularity of role-playing games. Try new games that challenge your left hemisphere, such as pool.

Act out
At its best, play is discovery—and what you discover through improvisation is your inner actor, who can try on many roles. (Believe it or not, a number of outstanding comedians started their careers as accountants.) You will be surprised to see that such play expands your behavioral repertoire—your brain has immense stored potential for enhancing your personality and leadership capacities. You can even experiment in meetings. Trying out different ways of interacting with colleagues, for example, increases cognitive fitness.

Find what you're not learning
If you're like most executives, you tend to ask very similar questions day to day in your professional and personal lives. So listen to yourself and figure out

what you *don't* seek. Asking a promising young subordinate what she thinks is a good place to start. Or vary your reading list. If you normally throw yourself into history and biography, try literary fiction; if it's mostly thrillers, try science.

Get the most out of business trips
Travel provides excellent opportunities for jolting your brain. Your time investment need not be too intensive. Visit a museum; read a novel set in the city you are visiting; devote a couple of hours to talking with locals around town. These activities not only increase your cultural IQ—they are also a good form of cognitive exercise.

Take notes—and then go back and read them
One of the world's greatest entrepreneurs, Richard Branson, carries a bound book with blank pages wherever he goes. Every time he sees or hears something interesting and new, he jots it down. He says that many of these ideas have become new businesses.

Try new technologies
Playing with that new touch screen and downloading that goofy video from YouTube on your iGadget to display on your megascreen TV activates innumerable brain channels linking your auditory, visual, and tactile networks with your limbic system and your prefrontal cortex. Talking about it and sharing your emotional energy with your friends will extend the activity throughout the brain. Even your brain stem, which keeps you wakeful and engaged, will get a workout.

Learn a new language or instrument
Studying a new language puts you at the pinnacle of mental athleticism. Learning a musical instrument or really playing that old clarinet in the closet gives your brain a big boost, too. Take lessons.

Exercise, exercise, exercise
Your brain is not an island—it is part of a system that benefits from cardiovascular exercise, good diet, and proper sleep habits. One of the most consistently identified defenses against developing Alzheimer's disease is a good exercise regimen. Very specific beneficial biochemical changes, such as increases in endorphins and cortisol, result from both cardiovascular and strength training. Those benefits literally flow through your blood vessels and reach your muscles, your joints, your bones, and, yes, your brain.

adult takes up painting—any time people look at and experience the world in a novel way—the right hemisphere is exercised. Later, the new knowledge (language, for instance) migrates to the left, exploitative hemisphere, where it is organized, encoded, and made available for day-to-day retrieval and use. If the left hemisphere is about language expression, then the right is about language acquisition.

As on the left side, the neural networks on the right benefit from exercise. The more new things you learn, the better you become at learning. Actively engaging in novel, challenging activities capitalizes on your capacity for neuroplasticity—the ability of your brain to reorganize itself adaptively and enhance its performance. Studies of older adults usually show that those who live this way possess more complex neural networks than those who do not. The people who remain engaged in life consistently display an attitude of openness to new and unexpected experiences. Abraham Goldstein followed such a regimen of cognitive fitness. As a lawyer living in Manhattan and a professor emeritus at Baruch College, Goldstein continued to tutor law students and lead a physically and mentally active life to the age of 103.

Continuous learning can provide another important benefit. Research shows that the Abraham Goldsteins of this world are more resistant to Alzheimer's disease and other forms of dementia. Take the case of Richard Wetherill, a retired university lecturer and a talented chess player who could think eight moves ahead. In early 2001, Wetherill noticed that his chess ability had diminished; he could see only five moves ahead. Convinced that this was a signal that something was wrong with him, he consulted a neurologist. He took the usual diagnostic tests and passed them all. His brain scans looked quite normal. He died two years later, and an autopsy was conducted. Postmortem brain pathology showed that Wetherill had suffered from advanced-stage Alzheimer's, which would have rendered most individuals cognitively nonfunctional. Wetherill's case illustrates how those who are cognitively fit thanks to vigorous intellectual stimulation can be protected from the mental decline that comes with age.

People who are receptive to novelty and innovation also tend to be good in a crisis, because they are open to seeing opportunity in even the direst situations. Gene Krantz's reaction to the darkest moment of the *Apollo 13* emergency is a case in point: "I believe this will be our finest hour." Krantz had a long history of challenging convention, policy, and practice at NASA. He organized special teams that drew talent out of traditional silos and across boundaries. He also gave outside vendors office space in his complex to build expertise and relationships. He was featured in Michael Useem's book *The Leadership Moment* as a paragon of effective creative leadership. There's no way to verify this without neural imaging, but we would expect Krantz's brain to have a highly connected network of neural pathways in the right hemisphere. His mind-set and experiences lead to the kind of right-hemisphere development that is so critical to cognitive fitness.

More generally, what we're talking about is having an open attitude that Buddhist monks refer to as the beginner's mind, a willingness to step back from prior knowledge and existing conventions in order to start over and cultivate new options—a challenge that typically activates right-hemisphere cognitions. If you are really serious about creating innovative options, you couldn't do better than to turn to Buddhist thinking. In *Zen Mind, Beginner's Mind,* Shunryu Suzuki describes the Zen mind as one that is open, allowing for both doubt and possibility, and one that has the ability to see things as fresh and new. As he observed, "In the beginner's mind there are many possibilities, but in the expert's there are few."

We also advocate adopting a protégé. While it's widely known that being a protégé benefits rising executives, an ongoing stream of research reveals that the person who often gets the most value from a mentoring relationship is the mentor, who is exposed to information, queries, and ideas from which she may otherwise be too remote. In the field of medicine, for example, senior attending physicians can learn a lot from the insightful questions raised by students.

Cognitive fitness can affect every part of your life. On an organizational level, it may be the ultimate lever for sustainable competitive advantage. Your critical task as a leader is to promote the highest levels of organizational performance by creating environments where people can achieve their brains' full potential. Thinking through the four steps and deciding how they apply to the strategic challenges your company faces is a good way to begin. Not all companies will come up with exactly the same mix of practices and policies; the cognitive profile required by a large company in the automobile industry may differ from what you'd need to run a biotech start-up. The former might emphasize left-hemisphere activity (for example, spotting hidden patterns in demand), while the latter might call mainly for right-hemisphere activity (for example, coping with a series of failed R&D projects). Whatever the best approach for your organization may be, a brain-positive culture that encourages people to put their whole brains to work can become a reality only with the right kind of committed leadership. The future belongs to companies with leaders who develop cognitive fitness for themselves and their organizations. CEOs need to be cognitive coaches to those whose work and decisions collectively create and propel the company's strategy.

Originally published in November 2007. Reprint R0711B

The Making of a Corporate Athlete

by Jim Loehr and Tony Schwartz

IF THERE IS ONE QUALITY that executives seek for themselves and their employees, it is sustained high performance in the face of ever-increasing pressure and rapid change. But the source of such performance is as elusive as the fountain of youth. Management theorists have long sought to identify precisely what makes some people flourish under pressure and others fold. We maintain that they have come up with only partial answers: rich material rewards, the right culture, management by objectives.

The problem with most approaches, we believe, is that they deal with people only from the neck up, connecting high performance primarily with cognitive capacity. In recent years there has been a growing focus on the relationship between emotional intelligence and high performance. A few theorists have addressed the spiritual dimension—how deeper values and a sense of purpose influence performance. Almost no one has paid any attention to the role played by physical capacities. A successful approach to sustained high performance, we have found, must pull together all of these elements and consider the person as a whole. Thus, our integrated theory of performance management addresses the body, the emotions, the mind, and the spirit. We call this hierarchy the *performance pyramid*. Each of its levels profoundly influences the others, and failure to address any one of them compromises performance.

Our approach has its roots in the two decades that Jim Loehr and his colleagues at LGE spent working with world-class athletes. Several years ago, the two of us began to develop a more comprehensive version of these techniques for executives facing unprecedented demands in the workplace. In effect, we realized, these executives are "corporate athletes." If they were to perform at high levels over the long haul, we posited, they would have to train in the same systematic, multilevel way that world-class athletes do. We have now tested our model on thousands of executives. Their dramatically improved work performance and their enhanced health and happiness confirm our initial hypothesis. In the pages that follow, we describe our approach in detail.

Ideal Performance State

In training athletes, we have never focused on their primary skills—how to hit a serve, swing a golf club, or shoot a basketball. Likewise, in business we don't address primary competencies such as public speaking, negotiating, or analyzing a balance sheet. Our efforts aim instead to help executives build their capacity for what might be called supportive or secondary competencies, among them endurance, strength, flexibility, self-control, and focus. Increasing capacity at all levels allows athletes and executives alike to bring their talents and skills to full ignition and to sustain high performance over time—a condition we call the *Ideal Performance State* (IPS). Obviously, executives can perform successfully even if they smoke, drink and weigh too much, or lack emotional skills or a higher purpose for working. But they cannot perform to their full potential or without a cost over time—to themselves, to their families, and to the corporations for which they work. Put simply, the best long-term performers tap into positive energy at all levels of the performance pyramid.

Extensive research in sports science has confirmed that the capacity to mobilize energy on demand is the foundation of IPS. Our own work has demonstrated that effective energy management has two key components. The first is the rhythmic movement between energy expenditure (stress) and energy renewal (recovery), which we term "oscillation." In the living laboratory of sports, we learned that the real enemy of high performance is not stress, which, paradoxical as it may seem, is actually the stimulus for growth. Rather, the problem is the absence of disciplined, intermittent recovery. Chronic stress without recovery depletes energy reserves, leads to burnout and breakdown, and ultimately undermines performance. Rituals that promote oscillation—rhythmic stress and recovery—are the second component of high performance. Repeated regularly, these highly precise, consciously developed routines become automatic over time.

The same methods that enable world-class athletes to reach IPS under pressure, we theorized, would be at least equally effective for business leaders—and perhaps even more important in their lives. The demands on executives to sustain high performance day in and day out, year in and year out, dwarf the challenges faced by any athlete we have ever trained. The average professional athlete, for example, spends most of his time practicing and only a small percentage—several hours a day, at most—actually competing. The typical executive, by contrast, devotes almost no time to training and must perform on demand ten, 12, 14 hours a day or more. Athletes enjoy several months of off-season, while most executives are fortunate to get three or four weeks of vacation a year. The career of the average professional athlete spans seven years; the average executive can expect to work 40 to 50 years.

Of course, even corporate athletes who train at all levels will have bad days and run into challenges they can't overcome. Life is tough, and for many time-starved executives, it is only getting tougher. But that is precisely our point. While it isn't always in our power to change our external conditions, we can train to better manage our inner state. We aim to help corporate athletes use the full range of their capacities to thrive in the most difficult circumstances and to emerge from stressful periods stronger, healthier, and eager for the next challenge.

Physical Capacity

Energy can be defined most simply as the capacity to do work. Our training process begins at the physical level because the body is our fundamental source of energy—the foundation of the performance pyramid. Perhaps the best paradigm for building capacity is weight lifting. Several decades of sports science research have established that the key to increasing physical strength is a phenomenon known as supercompensation—essentially the creation of balanced work-rest ratios. In weight lifting, this involves stressing a muscle to the point where its fibers literally start to break down. Given an adequate period of recovery (typically at least 48 hours), the muscle will not only heal, it will grow stronger. But persist in stressing the muscle without rest and the result will be acute and chronic damage. Conversely, failure to stress the muscle results in weakness and atrophy. (Just think of an arm in a cast for several weeks.) In both cases, the enemy is not stress, it's linearity—the failure to oscillate between energy expenditure and recovery.

We first understood the power of rituals to prompt recovery by observing world-class tennis players in the crucible of match play. The best competitors, we discovered, use precise recovery rituals in the 15 or 20 seconds *between* points—often without even being aware of it. Their between-point routines include concentrating on the strings of their rackets to avoid distraction, assuming a confident posture, and visualizing how they want the next point to play out. These routines have startling physiological effects. When we hooked players up to heart rate monitors during their matches, the competitors with the most consistent rituals showed dramatic oscillation, their heart rates rising rapidly during play and then dropping as much as 15% to 20% between points.

The mental and emotional effects of precise between-point routines are equally significant. They allow players to avoid negative feelings, focus their minds, and prepare for the next point. By contrast, players who lack between-point rituals, or who practice them inconsistently, become linear—they expend too much energy without recovery. Regardless of their talent or level of fitness, they become more vulnerable to frustration, anxiety, and loss of concentration and far more likely to choke under pressure.

The same lesson applies to the corporate athletes we train. The problem, we explain, is not so much that their lives are increasingly stressful as that they are so relentlessly linear. Typically, they push themselves too hard mentally and emotionally and too little physically. Both forms of linearity undermine performance.

When we began working with Marilyn Clark, a managing director of Salomon Smith Barney, she had almost no oscillation in her life. Clark, who is in her late 30s, runs the firm's Cleveland office. She is also the mother of three young children, and her husband is a high-powered executive in his own right. To all appearances, Clark lives an enviable life, and she was loath to complain about it. Yet her hectic lifestyle was exacting a cost, which became clear after some probing. In the mornings, temporarily fueled by coffee and a muffin, she was alert and energetic. By the afternoon, though, her energy sagged, and she got through the rest of the day on sheer willpower. At lunchtime, when she could have taken a few quiet moments to recover, she found that she couldn't say no to employees who lined up at her office seeking counsel and support. Between the demands of her job, her colleagues, and her family, she had almost no time for herself. Her frustration quietly grew.

We began our work with Clark by taking stock of her physical capacity. While she had been a passionate athlete as a teenager and an All-American lacrosse player in college, her fitness regimen for the past several years had been limited to occasional sit-ups before bedtime. As she learned more about the relationship between energy and high performance, Clark agreed that her first priority was to get back in shape. She wanted to feel better physically, and she knew from past experience that her mood would improve if she built regular workouts into her schedule.

Because old habits die hard, we helped Clark establish positive rituals to replace them. Part of the work was creating a supportive environment. The colleagues with whom Clark trained became a source of cheerleading—and even nagging—as she established a routine that would have previously seemed unthinkable. Clark committed to work out in a nearby gym three days a week, precisely at 1 p.m. She also enlisted her husband to watch the kids so that she could get in a workout on Saturdays and Sundays.

The High-Performance Pyramid

PEAK PERFORMANCE IN BUSINESS has often been presented as a matter of sheer brainpower, but we view performance as a pyramid. Physical well-being is its foundation. Above that rests emotional health, then mental acuity, and at the top, a sense of purpose. The Ideal Performance State—peak performance under pressure—is achieved when all levels are working together.

Rituals that promote oscillation—the rhythmic expenditure and recovery of energy—link the levels of the pyramid. For instance, vigorous exercise can produce a sense of emotional well-being, clearing the way for peak mental performance.

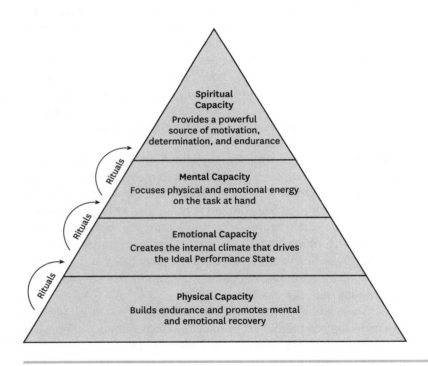

Regular workouts have helped Clark create clear work-life boundaries and restored her sense of herself as an athlete. Now, rather than tumbling into an energy trough in the afternoons and reaching for a candy bar, Clark returns to the office from her workouts feeling reenergized and better able to focus. Physical stress has become a source not just of greater endurance but also of emotional and mental recovery; Clark finds that she can work fewer hours and get more done. And finally, because she no longer feels chronically overburdened, she believes that she has become a better boss. "My body feels reawakened," she says. "I'm much more relaxed, and the resentment I was feeling about all the demands on me is gone."

Clark has inspired other members of her firm to take out health club memberships. She and several colleagues are subsidizing employees who can't easily afford the cost. "We're not just talking to each other about business accolades and who is covering which account," she says. "Now it's also about whether we got our workouts in and how well we're recovering. We're sharing something healthy, and that has brought people together."

The corporate athlete doesn't build a strong physical foundation by exercise alone, of course. Good sleeping and eating rituals are integral to effective energy management. When we first met Rudy Borneo, the vice chairman of Macy's West, he complained of erratic energy levels, wide mood swings, and difficulty concentrating. He was also overweight. Like many executives—and most Americans—his eating habits were poor. He typically began his long, travel-crammed days by skipping breakfast—the equivalent of rolling to the start line of the Indianapolis 500 with a near-empty fuel tank. Lunch was catch-as-catch-can, and Borneo used sugary snacks to fight off his inevitable afternoon hunger pangs. These foods spiked his blood glucose levels, giving him a quick jolt of energy, but one that faded quickly. Dinner was often a rich, multicourse meal eaten late in the evening. Digesting that much food disturbed Borneo's sleep and left him feeling sluggish and out of sorts in the mornings.

Sound familiar?

As we did with Clark, we helped Borneo replace his bad habits with positive rituals, beginning with the way he ate. We explained that by eating lightly but often, he could sustain a steady level of energy. (For a fuller account of the foundational exercise, eating, and sleep routines, see the sidebar "A Firm Foundation.") Borneo now eats breakfast every day—typically a high-protein drink rather than coffee and a bagel. We also showed him research by chronobiologists suggesting that the body and mind need recovery every 90 to 120 minutes. Using that cycle as the basis for his eating schedule, he installed a refrigerator by his desk and began eating five or six small but nutritious meals a day and sipping water frequently. He also shifted the emphasis in his workouts to interval training, which increased his endurance and speed of recovery.

In addition to prompting weight loss and making him feel better, Borneo's nutritional and fitness rituals have had a dramatic effect on other aspects of his life. "I now exercise for my mind as much as for my body," he says. "At the age of 59, I have more energy than ever, and I can sustain it for a longer period of time. For me, the rituals are the holy grail. Using them to create balance has had an impact on every aspect of my life: staying more positive, handling difficult human resource issues, dealing with change, treating people better. I really do believe that when you learn to take care of yourself, you free up energy and enthusiasm to care more for others."

Emotional Capacity

The next building block of IPS is emotional capacity—the internal climate that supports peak performance. During our early research, we asked hundreds of athletes to describe how they felt when they were performing at their best. Invariably, they used words such as "calm," "challenged," "engaged," "focused," "optimistic," and "confident." As sprinter Marion Jones put it shortly after winning one of her gold medals at the Olympic Games in Sydney: "I'm out here having a ball. This is not a stressful time in my life. This is a very happy time." When we later asked the same question of law enforcement officers, military personnel, surgeons, and corporate executives, they used remarkably similar language to describe their Ideal Performance State.

Just as positive emotions ignite the energy that drives high performance, negative emotions—frustration, impatience, anger, fear, resentment, and sadness—drain energy. Over time, these feelings can be literally toxic, elevating heart rate and blood pressure, increasing muscle tension, constricting vision, and ultimately crippling performance. Anxious, fear ridden athletes are far more likely to choke in competition, for example, while anger and frustration sabotage their capacity for calm focus.

The impact of negative emotions on business performance is subtler but no less devastating. Alan, an executive at an investment company, travels frequently, overseeing a half-dozen offices around the country. His colleagues and subordinates, we learned, considered him to be a perfectionist and an often critical boss whose frustration and impatience sometimes boiled over into angry tirades. Our work focused on helping Alan find ways to manage his emotions more effectively. His anger, we explained, was a reactive emotion, a fight-or-flight response to situations he perceived as threatening. To manage more effectively, he needed to transform his inner experience of threat under stress into one of challenge.

A regular workout regimen built Alan's endurance and gave him a way to burn off tension. But because his fierce travel schedule often got in the way of his workouts, we also helped him develop a precise five-step ritual to contain his negative emotions whenever they threatened to erupt. His initial challenge was to become more aware of signals from his body that he was on edge—physical tension, a racing heart, tightness in his chest. When he felt those sensations arise, his first step was to close his eyes and take several deep breaths. Next, he consciously relaxed the muscles in his face. Then, he made an effort to soften his voice and speak more slowly. After that, he tried to put himself in the shoes of the person who was the target of his anger—to imagine what he or she must be feeling. Finally, he focused on framing his response in positive language.

Instituting this ritual felt awkward to Alan at first, not unlike trying to learn a new golf swing. More than once he reverted to his old behavior. But within several weeks, the five-step drill had become automatic—a highly reliable way to short-circuit his reactivity.

A Firm Foundation

HERE ARE OUR BASIC STRATEGIES FOR renewing energy at the physical level. Some of them are so familiar they've become background noise, easy to ignore. That's why we're repeating them. If any of these strategies aren't part of your life now, their absence may help account for fatigue, irritability, lack of emotional resilience, difficulty concentrating, and even a flagging sense of purpose.

1. Actually do all those healthy things you know you ought to do

Eat five or six small meals a day; people who eat just one or two meals a day with long periods in between force their bodies into a conservation mode, which translates into slower metabolism. Always eat breakfast: eating first thing in the morning sends your body the signal that it need not slow metabolism to conserve energy. Eat a balanced diet. Despite all the conflicting nutritional research, overwhelming evidence suggests that a healthy dietary ratio is 50% to 60% complex carbohydrates, 25% to 35% protein, and 20% to 25% fat. Dramatically reduce simple sugars. In addition to representing empty calories, sugar causes energy-depleting spikes in blood glucose levels. Drink four to five 12-ounce glasses of water daily, even if you don't feel thirsty. As much as half the population walks around with mild chronic dehydration. And finally, on the "you know you should" list: get physically active. We strongly recommend three to four 20- to 30-minute cardiovascular workouts a week, including at least two sessions of intervals—short bursts of intense exertion followed by brief recovery periods.

2. Go to bed early and wake up early

Night owls have a much more difficult time dealing with the demands of today's business world, because typically, they still have to get up with the early

Numerous employees reported that he had become more reasonable, more approachable, and less scary. Alan himself says that he has become a far more effective manager.

Through our work with athletes, we have learned a number of other rituals that help to offset feelings of stress and restore positive energy. It's no coincidence, for example, that many athletes wear headphones as they prepare for competition. Music has powerful physiological and emotional effects. It can prompt a shift in mental activity from the rational left hemisphere of the brain to the more intuitive right hemisphere. It also provides a relief from obsessive thinking and worrying. Finally, music can be a means of directly birds. They're often groggy and unfocused in the mornings, dependent on caffeine and sugary snacks to keep up their energy. You can establish new sleep rituals. Biological clocks are not fixed in our genes.

3. Maintain a consistent bedtime and wake-up time

As important as the number of hours you sleep (ideally seven to eight) is the consistency of the recovery wave you create. Regular sleep cycles help regulate your other biological clocks and increase the likelihood that the sleep you get will be deep and restful.

4. Seek recovery every 90 to 120 minutes

Chronobiologists have found that the body's hormone, glucose, and blood pressure levels drop every 90 minutes or so. By failing to seek recovery and overriding the body's natural stress-rest cycles, overall capacity is compromised. As we've learned from athletes, even short, focused breaks can promote significant recovery. We suggest five sources of restoration: eat something, hydrate, move physically, change channels mentally, and change channels emotionally.

5. Do at least two weight-training workouts a week

No form of exercise more powerfully turns back the markers of age than weight training. It increases strength, retards osteoporosis, speeds up metabolism, enhances mobility, improves posture, and dramatically increases energy.

regulating energy—raising it when the time comes to perform and lowering it when it is more appropriate to decompress.

Body language also influences emotions. In one well-known experiment, actors were asked to portray anger and then were subjected to numerous physiological tests, including heart rate, blood pressure, core temperature, galvanic skin response, and hormone levels. Next, the actors were exposed to a situation that made them genuinely angry, and the same measurements were taken. There were virtually no differences in the two profiles. Effective acting produces precisely the same physiology that real emotions do. All great athletes understand this instinctively. If they carry themselves confidently, they will eventually start to feel confident, even in highly stressful situations. That's why we train our corporate clients to "act as if"—consciously creating the look on the outside that they want to feel on the inside. "You are what you repeatedly do," said Aristotle. "Excellence is not a singular act but a habit."

Close relationships are perhaps the most powerful means for prompting positive emotions and effective recovery. Anyone who has enjoyed a happy family reunion or an evening with good friends knows the profound sense of safety and security that these relationships can induce. Such feelings are closely associated with the Ideal Performance State. Unfortunately, many of the corporate athletes we train believe that in order to perform up to expectations at work, they have no choice but to stint on their time with loved ones. We try to reframe the issue. By devoting more time to their most important relationships and setting clearer boundaries between work and home, we tell our clients, they will not only derive more satisfaction but will also get the recovery that they need to perform better at work.

Mental Capacity

The third level of the performance pyramid—the cognitive—is where most traditional performance-enhancement training is aimed. The usual approaches tend to focus on improving competencies by using techniques such as process reengineering and knowledge management or by learning to use more sophisticated technology. Our training aims to enhance our clients' cognitive capacities—most notably their focus, time management, and positive- and critical-thinking skills.

Focus simply means energy concentrated in the service of a particular goal. Anything that interferes with focus dissipates energy. Meditation, typically viewed as a spiritual practice, can serve as a highly practical means of training attention and promoting recovery. At this level, no guidance from a guru is required. A perfectly adequate meditation technique involves sitting quietly and breathing deeply, counting each exhalation, and starting over when you reach ten. Alternatively, you can choose a word to repeat each time you take a breath.

Practiced regularly, meditation quiets the mind, the emotions, and the body, promoting energy recovery. Numerous studies have shown, for example, that experienced meditators need considerably fewer hours of sleep than nonmeditators. Meditation and other non-cognitive disciplines can also slow brain wave activity and stimulate a shift in mental activity from the left hemisphere of the brain to the right. Have you ever suddenly found the solution to a vexing problem while doing something "mindless" such as jogging, working in the garden, or singing in the shower? That's the left-brain, right-brain shift at work—the fruit of mental oscillation.

Much of our training at this level focuses on helping corporate athletes to consciously manage their time and energy. By alternating periods of stress with renewal, they learn to align their work with the body's need for breaks every 90 to 120 minutes. This can be challenging for compulsive corporate achievers. Jeffrey Sklar, 39, managing director for institutional sales at the New York investment firm Gruntal & Company, had long been accustomed to topping his competitors by brute force—pushing harder and more relentlessly than anyone else. With our help, he built a set of rituals that ensured regular recovery and also enabled him to perform at a higher level while spending fewer hours at work.

Once in the morning and again in the afternoon, Sklar retreats from the frenetic trading floor to a quiet office, where he spends 15 minutes doing deep-breathing exercises. At lunch, he leaves the office—something he once would have found unthinkable—and walks outdoors for at least 15 minutes. He also works out five or six times a week after work. At home, he and his wife, Sherry, a busy executive herself, made a pact never to talk business after 8 p.m. They also swore off work on the weekends, and they have stuck to their vow for nearly two years. During each of those years, Sklar's earnings have increased by more than 65%.

For Jim Connor, the president and CEO of FootJoy, reprioritizing his time became a way not just to manage his energy better but to create more balance in his life and to revive his sense of passion. Connor had come to us saying that he felt stuck in a deep rut. "My feelings were muted so I could deal with the emotional pain of life," he explains. "I had smoothed out all the vicissitudes in my life to such an extent that oscillation was prohibited. I was not feeling life but repetitively performing it."

Connor had imposed on himself the stricture that he be the first person to arrive at the office each day and the last to leave. In reality, he acknowledged, no one would object if he arrived a little later or left a little earlier a couple of days a week. He realized it also made sense for him to spend one or two days a week working at a satellite plant 45 minutes nearer to his home than his main office. Doing so could boost morale at the second plant while cutting 90 minutes from his commute.

Immediately after working with us, Connor arranged to have an office cleared out at the satellite factory. He now spends at least one full day a week there, prompting a number of people at that office to comment to him about his increased availability. He began taking a golf lesson one morning a week, which also allowed for a more relaxed drive to his main office, since he commutes there after rush hour on golf days. In addition, he instituted a monthly getaway routine with his wife. In the evenings, he often leaves his office earlier in order to spend more time with his family.

Connor has also meticulously built recovery into his workdays. "What a difference these fruit and water breaks make," he says. "I set my alarm watch for 90 minutes to prevent relapses, but I'm instinctively incorporating this routine into my life and love it. I'm far more productive as a result, and the quality of my thought process is measurably improved. I'm also doing more on the big things at work and not getting bogged down in detail. I'm pausing more to think and to take time out."

Rituals that encourage positive thinking also increase the likelihood of accessing the Ideal Performance State. Once again, our work with top athletes has taught us the power of creating specific mental rituals to sustain positive energy. Jack Nicklaus, one of the greatest pressure performers in the history of golf, seems to have an intuitive understanding of the importance of both oscillation and rituals. "I've developed a regimen that allows me to move from peaks of concentration into valleys of relaxation and back again as necessary," he wrote in *Golf Digest.* "My focus begins to sharpen as I walk onto the tee and steadily intensifies . . . until I hit [my drive]. . . . I descend into a valley as I leave the tee, either through casual conversation with a fellow competitor or by letting my mind dwell on whatever happens into it."

Visualization is another ritual that produces positive energy and has palpable performance results. For example, Earl Woods taught his son Tiger—Nicklaus's heir apparent—to form a mental image of the ball rolling into the hole before each shot. The exercise does more than produce a vague feeling of optimism and well-being. Neuroscientist Ian Robertson of Trinity College, Dublin, author of *Mind Sculpture,* has found that visualization can literally reprogram the neural circuitry of the brain, directly improving performance. It is hard to imagine a better illustration than diver Laura Wilkinson. Six months before the summer Olympics in Sydney, Wilkinson broke three toes on her right foot while training. Unable to go in the water because of her cast, she instead spent hours a day on the diving platform, visualizing each of her dives. With only a few weeks to actually practice before the Olympics, she pulled off a huge upset, winning the gold medal on the ten-meter platform.

Visualization works just as well in the office. Sherry Sklar has a ritual to prepare for any significant event in her work life. "I always take time to sit down in advance in a quiet place and think about what I really want from the meeting," she says. "Then I visualize myself achieving the outcome I'm after." In effect, Sklar is building mental muscles—increasing her strength, endurance, and flexibility. By doing so, she decreases the likelihood that she will be distracted by negative thoughts under pressure. "It has made me much more relaxed and confident when I go into presentations," she says.

Spiritual Capacity

Most executives are wary of addressing the spiritual level of the performance pyramid in business settings, and understandably so. The word "spiritual" prompts conflicting emotions and doesn't seem immediately relevant to high performance. So let's be clear: by spiritual capacity, we simply mean the energy that is unleashed by tapping into one's deepest values and defining a strong sense of purpose. This capacity, we have found, serves as sustenance in the face of adversity and as a powerful source of motivation, focus, determination, and resilience.

Consider the case of Ann, a high-level executive at a large cosmetics company. For much of her adult life, she has tried unsuccessfully to quit smoking, blaming her failures on a lack of self-discipline. Smoking took a visible toll on her health and her productivity at work—decreased endurance from shortness of breath, more sick days than her colleagues, and nicotine cravings that distracted her during long meetings.

Four years ago, when Ann became pregnant, she was able to quit immediately and didn't touch a cigarette until the day her child was born, when she began smoking again. A year later, Ann became pregnant for a second time, and again she stopped smoking, with virtually no symptoms of withdrawal. True to her pattern, she resumed smoking when her child was born. "I don't understand it," she told us plaintively.

We offered a simple explanation. As long as Ann was able to connect the impact of smoking to a deeper purpose—the health of her unborn child—quitting was easy. She was able to make what we call a "values-based adaptation." But without a strong connection to a deeper sense of purpose, she went back to smoking—an expedient adaptation that served her short-term interests. Smoking was a sensory pleasure for Ann, as well as a way to allay her anxiety and manage social stress. Understanding cognitively that it was unhealthy, feeling guilty about it on an emotional level, and even experiencing its negative effects physically were all insufficient motivations to change her behavior. To succeed, Ann needed a more sustaining source of motivation.

Making such a connection, we have found, requires regularly stepping off the endless treadmill of deadlines and obligations to take time for reflection. The inclination for busy executives is to live in a perpetual state of triage, doing whatever seems most immediately pressing while losing sight of any bigger picture. Rituals that give people the opportunity to pause and look inside include meditation, journal writing, prayer, and service to others. Each of these activities can also serve as a source of recovery—a way to break the linearity of relentless goal-oriented activity.

Taking the time to connect to one's deepest values can be extremely rewarding. It can also be painful, as a client we'll call Richard discovered. Richard is a stockbroker who works in New York City and lives in a distant suburb, where his wife stays at home with their three young children. Between his long commute and his long hours, Richard spent little time with his family. Like so many of our clients, he typically left home before his children woke up and returned around 7:30 in the evening, feeling exhausted and in no mood to talk to anyone. He wasn't happy with his situation, but he saw no easy solution. In time, his unhappiness began to affect his work, which made him even more negative when he got home at night. It was a vicious cycle.

One evening while driving home from work, Richard found himself brooding about his life. Suddenly, he felt so overcome by emotion that he stopped his car at a park ten blocks from home to collect himself. To his astonishment, he began to weep. He felt consumed with grief about his life and filled with longing for his family. After ten minutes, all Richard wanted to do was get home and hug his wife and children. Accustomed to giving their dad a wide berth at the end of the day, his kids were understandably bewildered when he walked in that evening with tears streaming down his face and wrapped them all in hugs. When his wife arrived on the scene, her first thought was that he'd been fired.

The next day, Richard again felt oddly compelled to stop at the park near his house. Sure enough, the tears returned and so did the longing. Once again, he rushed home to his family. During the subsequent two years, Richard was able to count on one hand the number of times that he failed to stop at the same location for at least ten minutes. The rush of emotion subsided over time, but his sense that he was affirming what mattered most in his life remained as strong as ever.

Richard had stumbled into a ritual that allowed him both to disengage from work and to tap into a profound source of purpose and

meaning—his family. In that context, going home ceased to be a burden after a long day and became instead a source of recovery and
renewal. In turn, Richard's distraction at work diminished, and he
became more focused, positive, and productive—so much so that he
was able to cut down on his hours. On a practical level, he created a
better balance between stress and recovery. Finally, by tapping into
a deeper sense of purpose, he found a powerful new source of energy for both his work and his family.

In a corporate environment that is changing at warp speed, performing consistently at high levels is more difficult and more necessary
than ever. Narrow interventions simply aren't sufficient anymore.
Companies can't afford to address their employees' cognitive capacities while ignoring their physical, emotional, and spiritual well-
being. On the playing field or in the boardroom, high performance
depends as much on how people renew and recover energy as on
how they expend it, on how they manage their lives as much as on
how they manage their work. When people feel strong and resilient—
physically, mentally, emotionally, and spiritually—they perform better, with more passion, for longer. They win, their families win, and
the corporations that employ them win.

Originally published in January 2001. Reprint R0101H

Stress Can Be a Good Thing If You Know How to Use It

by Alia Crum and Thomas Crum

WITH ALL THE MEDIA AND MEDICAL ATTENTION on stress and its negative health impacts, it is easy to reach the conclusion that stress is irredeemably bad—something to be avoided as much as possible.

We have a different perspective. We believe that pursuing a "stress-free" life often causes more stress down the line—problems compound, and by failing to face our most intense challenges we never overcome them. Think about a time when you experienced substantial personal or professional growth, or a time when you performed at your highest level, such as finishing a race, building a business, or raising a child. What was it that motivated and fueled you to grow, learn, and improve during these times? We are willing to bet that those times invariably involved some stress or struggle.

Stress has many wonderful attributes. It reminds us that we care; it connects us directly with the most challenging and important aspects of our lives. We aren't suggesting that sustained stress does not take a toll, only that it can bring unexpected benefits, too, in the form of personal growth. Combining our years of experience conducting leadership seminars and teaching meditation and martial arts (Tom) and exploring empirical research in the area of psychology (Alia) we have found that individuals who adopt a "stress is enhancing" mind-set in their lives show greater work performance and fewer negative health symptoms than those who adopt a "stress-is-debilitating" lens. Drawing on our work and research with executives, students, Navy SEALs and professional athletes, we have devised a three-step approach to responding to pressure that we believe can help you harness the creative power of stress while minimizing its deleterious effects.

Step One: See It

The first step to transforming your response to stress is to "see" your stress. Rather than denying it, or dwelling upon it, we recommend simply naming or labeling the stress you are facing. For example, you might simply say to yourself: "I'm stressed about my son failing school." Or "I'm stressed about our year-end numbers." Or "I'm stressed about my husband's recent health diagnosis."

Neuroscience research by Matt Lieberman shows how just acknowledging your stress can move reactivity in your brain from the automatic and reactive centers to the more conscious and deliberate ones. In one study, participants in a brain scan were shown negative emotional images. When asked to label the emotion the images invoked, neural activity moved from the amygdala region (the seat of emotion) to the prefrontal cortex, the area of the brain in which we do our conscious and deliberate thinking. In other words, purposefully acknowledging stress lets you pause your visceral reaction, allowing you to choose a more enhancing response.

Another reason to acknowledge and "see" your stress is that evading it is counterproductive anyway. Our research with Peter Salovey and Shawn Achor has shown that individuals who view stress as debilitating tend to either over or under react to stress whereas those with a "stress is enhancing" mind-set have a more moderate cortisol response to stress and are more willing to seek out and be open to feedback during stress, which can help them learn and grow for the longer-term.

Mindfulness and other centering practices can help you acknowledge and transform how you are responding to duress. Each person reacts differently. Do you have a racing heart? Clenched muscles? Or are you in the minority who feel a sudden urge to fall asleep? What are your psychological reactions? To judge? Blame others (or yourself)? How about your behavioral reactions: Do you check out of the conversation all together? Rush to the refrigerator? Noticing these reactions releases us from their grip and helps shift our focus to pursuing more productive responses.

Step Two: Own It

The key to "owning" your stress is to recognize that we tend to stress more, and more intensely, about things that matter to us. Stress shows us that we care; that the stakes matter. Owning this realization unleashes positive motivation—because deep down we know that things that are important shouldn't always come easy. A metaphor we often use to describe this state is "It's just a cold, dark night on the side of Everest." If you were climbing Everest, you could imagine that there might be some cold, dark nights on your journey up. But what did you expect—that climbing Everest would be a walk in the park? Do you really expect that raising a child, running a business, living a life of impact would be easy? Owning your stress won't necessarily make those cold, dark nights go away but they will likely be a bit more tolerable as you discover a sense of motivation and meaning.

"In Navy SEAL training," former SEAL Commander Curt Cronin recently told us, "the leadership cadre designs situations that are exponentially more stressful, chaotic, and dynamic than any combat operation so that the teams learn to center [themselves] in the most arduous circumstances. When the stress of the training seems unbearable, we can own it, knowing that ultimately it is what we have chosen to do—to be a member of a team that can succeed in any mission."

Step Three: Use It

Contrary to what you might think, the body's stress response was not designed to kill us. In fact, the evolutionary goal of the stress response was to help boost the body and mind into enhanced functioning, to help us grow and meet the demands we face. When the body encounters stress, it pumps hormones such as adrenaline and dopamine which fuel the brain and body with blood and oxygen, a response which propels the individual into a state of increased energy, heightened alertness, and narrowed focus. Although the stress response can sometimes be detrimental, in many cases, stress hormones actually induce growth and release chemicals into the body that rebuild cells, synthesize proteins and enhance immunity, leaving the body even stronger and healthier than it was before. Researchers call this effect physiological thriving, and any athlete knows its rewards.

The issue, then, is not in the stress response itself but in how we channel or employ this response. Simply reframing your response to stress as something that is beneficial can be helpful. Researcher Jeremy Jamieson demonstrated that students asked to reframe pre-test anxiety as beneficial perform better on the exams. Harvard Business School professor Alison Wood Brooks has shown how reframing anxiety as excitement can improve performance on tasks such as negotiating and giving an important speech.

Sometimes, however, it is not so clear how best to use stress, especially with longer-term or more complicated situations. Consider an ongoing conflict with a spouse or a boss, a complex health condition or even the recent passing of a loved one. The key in these cases is to simply be open to the opportunities and learning inherent in the stress. Experiencing these challenges as an inherent part of our life-cycle—no one goes through life untouched by grief or heartbreak—can facilitate the acquisition of mental toughness, deeper social bonds, heightened awareness, new perspectives, a sense of mastery, greater appreciation for life, a sense of meaning, and strengthened priorities. Indeed, some leadership scholars—most notably Abraham Zaleznik—have drawn upon William James' concept of "twice-born" personalities to argue that great leaders share the common experience of working through traumatic episodes in their lives.

That's something the SEAL community has learned firsthand in recent years as its combat missions have increased. Commander Cronin recently told us, "After multiple years of back-to-back deployments, post-traumatic stress disorder continued to grow within the SEAL community. Learning about post-traumatic growth, learning to ask 'how could these experiences serve us?' and being pushed to own the experiences that we had been through and use them to fuel our future, proved a powerful tool in helping our individuals, teams and organization thrive, not in spite of the stress but because of it."

As a society we largely fail to frame stress as potentially enhancing and often miss opportunities to learn from and grow from stressful moments. That does not mean that we advocate viewing all stressors as a positive thing; but we do advocate that you embrace your stress response as a powerful tool for helping you overcome the inevitable challenges in life that can—and will—arise.

Originally published in September 2015. Reprint H02BK8

How to Bounce Back from Adversity

by Joshua D. Margolis and Paul G. Stoltz

THINGS ARE HUMMING ALONG, and then: A top client calls and says, "We're switching suppliers, starting next month. I'm afraid your company no longer figures into our plans." Or three colleagues, all of whom joined the organization around the same time you did, are up for promotion—but you aren't. Or your team loses another good person in a third round of layoffs; weak markets or no, you still need to make your numbers, but now you'll have to rely heavily on two of the most uncooperative members of the group.

So how do you react? Are you angry and disappointed, ranting and raving to anyone who will listen? Do you feel dejected and victimized, resigned to the situation even as you deny the cold reality of it? Or do you experience a rush of excitement—perhaps tinged with fear—because you sense an opportunity to develop your skills and talents in ways you'd never imagined? The truth is, you've probably reacted in all those ways when confronted with a challenge—maybe even cycling through multiple emotional states in the course of dealing with one really big mess.

Whatever your initial reaction, however, the challenge is to turn a negative experience into a productive one—that is, to counter adversity with resilience. Psychological resilience is the capacity to respond quickly and constructively to crises. It's a central dynamic in most survival stories, such as those of the shell-shocked individuals and organizations that rallied in the wake of 9/11 and Hurricane Katrina. But resilience can be hard to muster for many reasons: Fear, anger, and confusion can paralyze us after a severe setback. Assigning blame rather than generating solutions is an all-too-human tendency. Worse yet, those to whom we turn for counsel may offer us exactly the wrong kind of advice.

Decades of research in psychology, on topics including hardiness, learned helplessness, coping, and the correlation between cognitive style and health, confirms that each of us has a distinct, consistent pattern of thinking about life's twists and turns—a pattern of which most of us are largely unaware. It may be an unconscious reflex to look backward from traumatic incidents to explain what just happened. Such analysis can be useful, certainly—but only up to the point where strong negative emotions start to prevent our moving on.

We believe that managers can build high levels of resilience in themselves and their teams by taking charge of how they think about adversity. Resilient managers move quickly from analysis to a plan of action (and reaction). After the onset of adversity, they shift from cause-oriented thinking to response-oriented thinking, and their focus is strictly forward. In our work with leaders in a variety of companies and industries, we've identified four lenses through which managers can view adverse events to make this shift effectively.

- **Control.** When a crisis hits, do you look for what you can improve now rather than trying to identify all the factors—even those beyond your control—that caused it in the first place?

- **Impact.** Can you sidestep the temptation to find the origins of the problem in yourself or others and focus instead on identifying what positive effects your personal actions might have?

- **Breadth.** Do you assume that the underlying cause of the crisis is specific and can be contained, or do you worry that it might cast a long shadow over all aspects of your life?

- **Duration.** How long do you believe that the crisis and its repercussions will last?

Idea in Brief

Psychological resilience—the capacity to respond quickly and constructively in a crisis—can be hard to muster when a manager is paralyzed by fear, anger, confusion, or a tendency to assign blame.

Resilient managers shift quickly from endlessly dissecting traumatic events to looking forward, determining the best course of action given new realities. They understand the size and scope of the crisis and the levels of control and impact they may have in a bad situation.

The authors describe a **resilience regimen**—a series of pointed questions designed to help managers replace negative responses with creative, resourceful ones and to move forward despite real or perceived obstacles.

The first two lenses characterize an individual's personal reaction to adversity, and the second two capture his or her impressions of the adversity's magnitude. Managers should consider all four to fully understand their instinctive responses to personal and professional challenges, setbacks, or failures.

In the following pages we'll describe a deliberative rather than reflexive approach to dealing with hardship—what we call a *resilience regimen*. By asking a series of pointed questions, managers can grasp their own and their direct reports' habits of thought and help reframe negative events in productive ways. With the four lenses as a guide, they can learn to stop feeling paralyzed by crisis, respond with strength and creativity, and help their direct reports do the same.

When Adversity Strikes

Most of us go with our gut when something bad happens. Deeply ingrained habits and beliefs sap our energy and keep us from acting constructively. People commonly fall into one of two emotional traps. One is *deflation*. Someone who has marched steadily through a string of successes can easily come to feel like a hero, able to fix any problem single-handedly. A traumatic event can snap that person back to reality. Even for the less heroic among us, adversity can touch off intense bursts of negative emotion—as if a dark cloud had settled behind our eyes, as one manager described it. We may feel disappointed in ourselves or others, mistreated and dispirited, even besieged.

That was the case with an executive we'll call Andrea, who headed up a major subsidiary of a U.S. automotive parts supplier. She had put up with years of internal bickering and the company's calcified cost structure. But over time she managed to bring the warring factions—unions, management, engineers, and marketers—together, and she gained widespread approval for a plan that would phase out old facilities and reduce crippling costs: Rather than try to supply every make and manufacturer, the company would focus on the truck market. Even more important, Andrea rallied everyone around a new line of products and a clear value proposition for customers that would rejuvenate the company's brand. The future looked bright.

Then fuel prices skyrocketed, the economy seized up, and demand from all segments of the truck market evaporated almost overnight. The recession had brought unfathomable challenges to the organization, and their suddenness left Andrea feeling as if she'd been socked in the stomach. After all her hard work, difficult conversations, and strategizing to fix the previous problems, she felt overmatched—for the first time in her career. Andrea lacked resilience precisely because she had a long history of wins.

The other emotional trap is *victimization*. Many of us assume the role of helpless bystander in the face of an adverse event. "Those people" have put us in an unfortunate position, we tell ourselves (and others) again and again. We dismiss both criticism and helpful suggestions from others, and go out of our way to affirm that we're right, everyone else is wrong, and no one understands us. Meanwhile, self-doubt may creep in, making us feel hopelessly constrained by circumstances.

Greg, a senior business development manager at an electronic accessories company, felt just this way. He had sailed through his first three years at the company with several promotions, taking on increasing responsibility—first for building brand awareness among younger consumers, and then for building new relationships (and gaining more shelf space) with large retailers throughout the United States and Canada. But as global competition heated up, Greg's peers and superiors asked him to rethink his approach and questioned whether retail outlets were still a viable distribution channel. Big-box stores were squeezing the company's margins, and physically servicing all the company's accounts seemed unnecessarily expensive compared with online options. Greg reacted to his colleagues' requests by becoming more and more defensive and extremely angry.

These stories illustrate the two-headed hydra of contemporary adversity. First, highly accomplished managers are confronting, in rapid succession, challenges the likes of which they've never seen before—a worldwide economic crisis, the globalization of business, the rise of new technologies, deep demographic shifts. Feeling discouraged and helpless, they turn away from the problem and, unfortunately, from people who might be able to help. Second, even if these managers went to their bosses for guidance, they'd most likely receive inadequate coaching. That's because most supervisors, riding their own long wave of hard-won successes, lack the empathy to intervene effectively. They may not know how to counsel direct reports they feel aren't quite as talented as they were at escaping the shadow of defeat. They may be so well accustomed to handling adversity in ways that minimize their psychological stress that they don't recognize their own bad habits. (See the sidebar "Coaching Resilience.")

The Capacity for Resilience

Independent studies in psychology and our own observations suggest that the ability to bounce back from adversity hinges on uncovering and untangling one's implicit beliefs about it—and shifting how one responds.

Most of us, when we experience a difficult episode, make quick assumptions about its causes, magnitude, consequences, and duration. We instantly decide, for example, whether it was inevitable, a function of forces beyond our control, or whether we could somehow have prevented it. Managers need to shift from this kind of reflexive thinking to "active" thinking about how best to respond,

Coaching Resilience

OFTEN EVEN THE MOST RESILIENT MANAGERS run into trouble trying to coach direct reports in crisis. They react with either a how-to pep talk delivered utterly without empathy or understanding, or a sympathetic ear and reassurance that things will turn out OK. Neither response will equip your team members to handle the next unforeseen twist or turn. Instead, you should adopt a collaborative, inquisitive approach that can help your direct reports generate their own options and possibilities.

Suppose a defensive employee were self-aware enough to ask you, his mentor, for help dealing with a professional setback—say, being passed over for promotion. You could just acknowledge his feelings and basically manage his response for him—outlining who he needs to talk to and in what order, and what to do if he doesn't get the answers he wants. But if you ask specifying, visualizing, and collaborating questions—such as "How can you step up to make the most immediate, positive impact on this situation?" and "How do you think your efforts in that direction would affect your team and your peers?"—you put the ball back in your employee's court. You're not endorsing any particular perspective, you're not providing absolute answers—you're helping to build resilience in a team member.

---

asking themselves what aspects they can control, what impact they can have, and how the breadth and duration of the crisis might be contained. Three types of questions can help them make this shift.

Specifying questions help managers identify ways to intervene; the more specific the answers, the better. *Visualizing questions* help shift their attention away from the adverse event and toward a more positive outcome. *Collaborating questions* push them to reach out to others—not for affirmation or commiseration but for joint problem solving. Each type of question can clarify each of the four lenses of resilient thinking.

Taken together, the four sets make up the resilience regimen. Let's take a closer look at each set in turn.

Control

According to multiple studies—including those by Bernard Weiner, of UCLA, and James Amirkhan, of Cal State Long Beach, and the classic University of Chicago study of executives by Suzanne Ouellette and Salvatore Maddi—our reactions to stressful situations depend on the degree of control we believe we can exercise. Andrea struggled with whether she could still contribute meaningfully to her company or whether the sudden shifts in the economy had moved the situation beyond her control. If Greg continued to attribute criticism of his retail strategy to "scheming peers," he might fail to see what he personally could do to influence the company's long-term strategy or his own destiny. The following questions can help managers identify ways to exercise control over what happens next:

Specifying: What aspects of the situation can I directly influence to change the course of this adverse event?

Visualizing: What would the manager I most admire do in this situation?

Collaborating: Who on my team can help me, and what's the best way to engage that person or those people?

The goal in asking these questions is not to come up with a final plan of action or an immediate understanding of how the team should react. Rather, it is to generate possibilities—to develop, in a disciplined and concrete way, an inventory of what *might* be done. (The next set of questions can help managers outline what *will* be done.) Had Andrea asked herself these three questions, she might have identified an opportunity to, say, rally the company around emerging safety and fuel-efficiency devices in the industry, or to use the slowdown to perfect the company's newer, still-promising products by working more closely with major customers. Similarly, if Greg had undertaken the exercise, he might have been able to channel something his mentor once told him: "It's not about whether I'm right or wrong. It's about what's best for the company." With that in mind, Greg might have clearly seen the benefits of reaching out to his peers and team members to assess alternative go-to-market approaches. The ingenuity and work ethic he had applied to building the retail business could have been turned to devising the next great strategy.

Impact

Related to our beliefs about whether we can turn things around are our assumptions about what caused a negative event: Did the problem originate with us personally, or somewhere else? Greg attributed the criticism of his retail distribution strategy to his "competitive, power-hungry" colleagues rather than to the possible shortcomings of his approach. He was too deeply mired in defensiveness to get out of his own way. Andrea felt powerless in the face of challenges she'd never before had to meet and forces that eclipsed her individual initiative and effort. Instead of giving in to deflation and victimization, managers can focus intently on how they might affect the event's outcome.

Specifying: How can I step up to make the most immediate, positive impact on this situation?

Visualizing: What positive effect might my efforts have on those around me?

Collaborating: How can I mobilize the efforts of those who are hanging back?

If he had focused on these questions, Greg might have seen that he was not simply being asked to discard his accounts and acknowledge that his strategy was misguided; rather, he was being cast as a potential player in the organization's change efforts. He might have appreciated that openly and rigorously assessing his business-development strategy could influence others—whether his assessment validated the status quo or led to a solution no one had thought of yet. And he might have reignited the entrepreneurial culture he so valued when he joined the company by soliciting others' input on the marketing strategy. For her part, Andrea knew all too well that her company's fortunes depended on economic conditions—but she couldn't see how her response to the market failures might energize the organization. These questions might have helped her.

Breadth

When we encounter a setback, we tend to assume that its causes are either specific to the situation or more broadly applicable, like poison that will taint everything we touch. To build up resilience, managers need to stop worrying about the reach of the causes and focus instead on how to limit the damage. These questions may even highlight opportunities in the midst of chaos.

A Change in Mind-Set

TO STRENGTHEN THEIR RESILIENCE, MANAGERS need to shift from reflex-ive, cause-oriented thinking to active, response-oriented thinking.

Cause-Oriented Thinking	Response-Oriented Thinking
CONTROL	
Was this adverse event inevitable, or could I have prevented it?	What features of the situation can I (even potentially) improve?
IMPACT	
Did I cause the adverse event, or did it result from external sources?	What sort of positive impact can I personally have on what happens next?
BREADTH	
Is the underlying cause of this event specific to it or more widespread?	How can I contain the negatives of the situation and generate currently unseen positives?
DURATION	
Is the underlying cause of this event enduring or temporary?	What can I do to begin addressing the problem now?

Specifying: What can I do to reduce the potential downside of this adverse event—by even 10%? What can I do to maximize the poten-tial upside—by even 10%?

Visualizing: What strengths and resources will my team and I de-velop by addressing this event?

Collaborating: What can each of us do on our own, and what can we do collectively, to contain the damage and transform the situa-tion into an opportunity?

These questions might have helped Andrea achieve two core ob-jectives. Instead of endlessly revisiting the repercussions of plum-meting truck sales, she might have identified large and small ways in which she and her team could use the economic crisis to reconfigure the company's manufacturing processes. And rather than fixating on how awful and extensive the damage to the organization was, she could have imagined a new postrecession norm—thriving in the face of tighter resources, more selective customers, and more exacting government scrutiny. Greg might have seen that he had a rare opportunity to gain valuable leadership skills and relevant insights about competitors' marketing strategies by engaging peers and team members in reassessing the retail strategy.

Duration

Some hardships in the workplace seem to have no end in sight—underperformance quarter after quarter, recurring clashes between people at different levels and in different parts of the company, a stalled economy. But questions about duration can put the brakes on such runaway nightmares. Here, though, it's important to begin by imagining the desired outcome.

Visualizing: What do I want life to look like on the other side of this adversity?

Specifying: What can I do in the next few minutes, or hours, to move in that direction?

Collaborating: What sequence of steps can we put together as a team, and what processes can we develop and adopt, to see us through to the other side of this hardship?

Greg was sure that criticism of his business-development approach signaled the end: no more promotions, no more recognition from higher-ups of his hard work and tangible results, nothing to look forward to but doing others' bidding in a company that was sowing the seeds of decline. These three questions might have broadened his outlook. That is, he might have seen the benefits of quickly arranging meetings with his mentor (for personal counsel) and with his team (for professional input on strategy). The questions could have been a catalyst for listing the data required to make a case for or against change, the analyses the team would need to run, and the questions about various sales channels and approaches that needed to be answered. This exercise might have helped Greg see a workable path through the challenge he was experiencing. The result would have been renewed confidence that he and his team could keep their company at the forefront of customer service.

The Research Behind the Resilience Regimen

TWO CONVERGING STREAMS OF RESEARCH informed our work. The first examines how patterns of understanding the world shape people's responses to stressful situations. Albert Ellis and Aaron Beck pioneered this research, followed by, among others, Martin Seligman and Christopher Peterson on learned helplessness; Richard Lazarus and Susan Folkman on coping; and Lyn Abramson, David Burns, and James Amirkhan on how "attributional styles" affect health. More recently, Karen Reivich and Andrew Shatté identified how people can strengthen their resilience.

The second stream, pioneered by Suzanne Ouellette and Salvatore Maddi in their studies of hardiness and extended most recently by Deborah Khoshaba and Aaron Antonovsky, explored what differentiated two groups of people who encountered intense stress. One group flourished while the other sank.

A common finding emerges from these two streams of inquiry: How people approach trying circumstances influences both their ability to deal with them and, ultimately, their own success and well-being.

Answering the Questions

Although the question sets offer a useful framework for retraining managers' responses, simply knowing what to ask isn't enough. You won't become more resilient simply because you've read this far and have made a mental note to pull out these questions the next time a destabilizing difficulty strikes. To strengthen your capacity for resilience, you need to internalize the questions by following two simple precepts:

Write down the answers

Various studies on stress and coping with trauma demonstrate that the act of writing about difficult episodes can enhance an individual's emotional and physical well-being. Indeed, writing offers people command over an adverse situation in a way that merely thinking about it does not. It's best to treat the resilience regimen as a timed exercise: Give yourself at least 15 minutes, uninterrupted, to write down your responses to the 12 questions. That may seem both too long and too short—too long because managers rarely have that much time for any activity, let alone one involving personal reflection. But you'll actually end up saving time. Instead of ruminating about events, letting them interrupt your work, you'll have solutions in the making. As you come to appreciate and rely on this exercise, 15 minutes may feel too short.

Do it every day

When you're learning any new skill, repetition is critical. The resilience regimen is a long-term fitness plan, not a crash diet. You must ask and answer these questions daily if they are to become second nature. But that can't happen if bad habits crowd out the questions. You don't need to experience a major trauma to practice; you can ask yourself the questions in response to daily annoyances that sap your energy—a delayed flight, a slow computer, an unresponsive colleague. You can use the four lenses in virtually any order, but it's important to start with your weakest dimension. If you tend to blame others and overlook your own potential to contribute, start with the impact questions. If you tend to worry that the adverse event will ruin everything, start with the breadth questions.

Under ongoing duress, executives' capacity for resilience is critical to maintaining their mental and physical health. Paradoxically, however, building resilience is best done precisely when times are most difficult—when we face the most upending challenges, when we are at the greatest risk of misfiring with our reactions, when we are blindest to the opportunities presented. All the more reason, then, to use the resilience regimen to tamp down unproductive responses to adversity, replace negativity with creativity and resourcefulness, and get things done despite real or perceived obstacles.

Originally published in January–February 2010. Reprint R1001E

Rebounding from Career Setbacks

by Mitchell Lee Marks, Philip Mirvis, and Ron Ashkenas

BRIAN WAS A RISING STAR at his company. He advanced through several senior management roles and was soon tapped to head a business unit, reporting directly to the CEO. But after about two years in the job, despite his stellar financial results, his boss suddenly dismissed him. Brian was told that the company was trying to be a more open, engaged, global enterprise and that his aggressive leadership style didn't reflect those values.

Like most ambitious managers who suffer career setbacks, Brian went through a period of shock, denial, and self-doubt. After all, he'd never previously failed in a position. He had trouble accepting the reality that he wasn't as good as he'd thought he was. He also felt upset and angry that his boss hadn't given him a chance to prove himself. Eventually, however, he recognized that he couldn't reverse the decision and chose to focus on moving forward. None of the people working for him had objected to his dismissal, so he was particularly keen to figure out how to foster loyalty in future employees.

Within a few months, a large industrial parts company impressed with Brian's undisputed ability to meet financial targets recruited him to lead a division. The job was a step down from his previous role, but he decided to take it so that he could experiment with different ways of working and leading, learning to better control his emotions and rally his team around him. It paid off: Less than three years later, yet another company—this time, a *Fortune* 500 manufacturer—hired him to be its CEO. During his seven-year tenure in that job, he doubled the firm's revenue and created a culture that balanced innovation with a disciplined focus on productivity and performance.

Of course, not everyone can go from being out of a job to running a large company. But in more than 30 years of research and consulting work with executive clients, we've found that one lesson from Brian's story applies pretty universally: Even a dramatic career failure can become a springboard to success if you respond in the right way. To execute a turnaround like Brian's, you focus on a few key tasks: Determine why you lost, identify new paths, and seize the right opportunity when it's within your reach.

Figure Out Why You Lost

We've interviewed hundreds of executives who have been fired, laid off, or passed over for promotion (as a result of mergers, restructurings, competition for top jobs, or personal failings). Often, we find them working through the classic stages of loss defined by psychiatrist Elisabeth Kübler-Ross: They start with shock and denial about the events and move on to anger at the company or the boss, bargaining over their fate, and then a protracted period of licking their wounds and asking themselves whether they can ever regain the respect of their peers and team. Many of them never make it to the "acceptance" stage.

That's partly because, as social psychologists have found in decades' worth of studies, high achievers usually take too much credit for their successes and assign too much external blame for their failures. It's a type of attribution bias that protects self-esteem but also prevents learning and growth. People focus on situational factors or company politics instead of examining their own role in the problem.

Some ask others for candid feedback, but most turn to sympathetic friends, family members, and colleagues who reinforce their self-image ("You deserved that job") and feed their sense of injustice

("You have every right to be angry"). This prevents them from considering their own culpability and breaking free of the destructive behavior that derailed them in the first place. It may also lead them to ratchet back their current efforts and future expectations in the workplace.

Those who rebound from career losses take a decidedly different approach. Instead of getting stuck in grief or blame, they actively explore how they contributed to what went wrong, evaluate whether they sized up the situation correctly and reacted appropriately, and consider what they would do differently if given the chance. They also gather feedback from a wide variety of people (including superiors, peers, and subordinates), making it clear that they want honest feedback, not consolation.

Brian, for example, had to engage in frank, somewhat painful conversations with his boss, several direct reports, and a few trusted colleagues to discover that he had developed a career-limiting reputation for being difficult and not always in control of his emotions.

Also consider Stan, a senior partner at a boutique professional services firm considering global expansion. A vocal proponent of the growth plan, he had hoped to lead the company's new London office. When another partner was selected instead, Stan was outraged. He stewed for a few weeks but then resolved to take a more productive tack. He set up one-on-one meetings with members of the firm's executive committee. At the start of each session, he explained that he wasn't trying to reverse the decision; he just wanted to understand why it had been made. He took care not to sound bitter or to bad-mouth the process or the people involved. He maintained a positive, confident tone, and he expressed a willingness to learn from his missteps.

As a result, the executive committee members gave him consistent, useful comments: They regarded his aggressiveness as an asset in the United States but worried that it would get in the way of securing new clients and running an office in the UK. His initial reaction was defensive. ("No one minded my aggressiveness when it landed key contracts," he thought.) But he kept those feelings in check—and quickly came around to appreciating the candor. "It wasn't that they were asking me to change," Stan reflected, "but they made clear to me that my style got in the way of this opportunity."

Identify New Paths

The next step is to objectively weight the potential for turning your loss into a win, whether that's a different role in your organization, a move to a new company, or a shift to a different industry or career.

Reframing losses as opportunities involves hard thinking about who you are and what you want. Research shows that escapism is a common reaction to career derailment—people may take trips to get away from their troubles, immerse themselves in busywork, drink or eat excessively, or avoid discussing their thoughts and plans with family and friends. While these behaviors can give you mental space to sort things out, they rarely lead to a productive transition. It's more effective to engage in a focused exploration of all the options available.

New opportunities don't usually present themselves right away, of course, and it can be hard to spot them through the fog of anger and disappointment in the early days after a setback. Studies by change management expert William Bridges highlight the tension people feel when they're torn between hanging onto their current identities and expectations and letting go. Leaders we've counseled describe entering a "twilight zone": The status quo has been fatally disrupted, but it's not clear yet what success will look like in the future.

That's why it's useful to take time to test out some ideas for what to do next. One option is to speak with a career counselor or engage in therapy, both to clarify goals and to work on personal development. Another is to take a temporary leave from your job to go back to school or test-drive a career interest at a start-up or a nonprofit. Pausing a bit can allow you to find new meaning in your setback.

Recall how Brian reacted when he was fired from his unit-head job: He began to consider lower-level positions that would give him room to tinker with his leadership style. Or look at Paula, whom we met while studying the resiliency of online advertising executives involved in restructurings. When her high-tech company's new CEO launched a corporate makeover, Paula felt relatively safe because the European business unit she led had met or exceeded its targets for 11 straight quarters, and she had been promoted three times in five years. But then she discovered that her position would be eliminated.

At first Paula blamed everything from company politics to her boss's failure to protect her and her team. Then, three months after the announcement, her last day arrived. She had no plans and didn't want to make any right away. Instead she spent time examining her life and her career. She reached out to friends and business associates—"not to network" (her words) but to gain perspective and advice in thinking through her goals. She reflected on each conversation, made notes, and eventually developed what she dubbed "four themes for my next job": She wanted to bring new products to market (rather than relaunching U.S. offerings in other regions), to interact more directly with clients, to work for a company with a unique value proposition, and to have colleagues she liked and trusted. Paula then tailored her job search to achieve those goals.

Seize the Right Opportunity

After you identify possible next steps, it's time to pick one. Admittedly, this can be a little frightening, especially if you're venturing into unknown career territory. Reimagining your professional identity is one thing; bringing it to life is another. Remember, though, that you haven't left your skills and experience behind with your last job, and you'll also bring with you the lessons learned from the setback. You may also have productively revised your definition of success.

Research we've conducted, along with career specialist Douglas (Tim) Hall, shows that needs and priorities can change dramatically over time—as children are born or grow up and move out, after a divorce or a parent's death, when early dreams fade in midlife and new ones emerge, and when perspectives and skills become outdated and new growth challenges beckon. So choosing the right opportunity has a lot to do with the moment when you happen to be looking.

Paula's story is a case in point. Her list of "must haves" led her to interview for and accept a more senior position, as VP of international sales, at a smaller firm in the same industry. The job was located in the European city where she already lived and wanted to stay.

Brian, by contrast, took a significant step down, but he took advantage of the opportunity to learn to become a better manager. He developed an understanding of the triggers that had caused him to behave unproductively in the past and devised coping strategies. For example, instead of immediately pouncing on subordinates for performance "misses," he learned to have off-line discussions with the relevant managers. After some practice, the measured approach began to feel more natural to him.

Bruce, a senior IT manager at a New York bank that went through a merger, is another example. He kept his job in the deal's aftermath but was devastated to lose out in his bid to become the chief technology officer of the merged company. He stayed on through the integration, but after a year of rethinking his personal and career goals—and considering a variety of jobs—he moved with his family to Austin, Texas, and joined a small technology firm that became wildly successful. Just as important, he also found time to coach his two children's soccer teams and pursue his passion for music as a guitarist for a local band.

Like Paula and Brian, Bruce did serious discovery work after his setback—and then acted with conviction. He moved to a new city, industry, and job that would allow him to recover and thrive.

For executives who decide to stay with their employers, the biggest change may be in mind-set or psychological commitment. That's what happened with Stan at the professional services firm: Having gained a clearer sense of how his colleagues viewed him, he embraced his role as rainmaker, better appreciating the income, status, and perks that came with it. He also found a new source of satisfaction and accomplishment: mentoring the next generation of talent on how to win new business.

Shifting perspective like this takes just as much energy as switching companies or jobs. If you're not able to dig into your current work with renewed gusto, as Stan did, you might decide to put more

Realizing What You're Made Of

by Glenn E. Mangurian

THOSE WHO HAVE SURVIVED a traumatic, life-altering event often convey a curious sentiment: They wouldn't have it any other way. Some people emerge from adversity—whether a career crisis or a devastating breakup or a frightening diagnosis—not just changed but stronger and more content. They seem to have found new peace and even an optimism that they didn't have before. It's tempting to dismiss this sort of response as making the best of a bad situation. Not long ago, I would have done so, too.

On May 26, 2001, I suffered an unprovoked disc rupture that pressed against my spinal cord, leaving the lower half of my body permanently paralyzed. I had two lengthy operations and spent two months of my life in a Boston rehabilitation hospital and four years in physical therapy. It was the kind of experience that nobody can anticipate. I was healthy and secure in my career as a management consultant, and in an instant, my life was utterly transformed and filled with uncertainty. At first, I was mostly frightened and in serious pain. Then, I felt anger and sadness at losing the use of my legs. Compounding those emotions was the recognition that it wasn't just my own life that would be severely altered: I had a wife and two children, whose lives would change forever and who would have to give up some of their own dreams.

Becoming paralyzed is without question the worst thing that has ever happened to me. I've had some very dark days, and life is a constant struggle. But at the same time, the experience has allowed me to take stock of all that I have, rediscover some of the neglected parts of my life, and cut through the clutter to focus on what really matters. Over the course of my hospital stay, I found the will to accept that my old life was gone and decided that I would create a new and equally meaningful one, drawing on all my experiences and a caring community of family and friends. Today, I've not just returned to consulting; I've also engaged in endeavors that wouldn't have occurred to me before, such as advocating for stem cell research.

It's a cliché to say that what doesn't kill you makes you stronger, and most people can accept that it's generally true. But more content? That's harder to explain. In my case, in spite of the frustrations of being in a wheelchair, I can honestly say that my life is good and that I am more at peace than I was before. How can that be? I know I was lucky that my injury didn't kill me and that I had resources to draw on, but I also believe that we are born with a renewable capacity for resilience—a built-in power to heal, regenerate, and grow beyond our known limits.

Resilience is one of the key qualities desired in business leaders today, but many people confuse it with toughness. Toughness is an aspect of resilience, certainly, as it enables people to separate emotion from the negative consequences of difficult choices. It can be an advantage in business, but only to a point. That's because it can create an armor that deflects emotion, and it can cut you off from many of the resources needed to bounce back—notably, the people around you. Resilience, by contrast, is not about deflecting challenges but about absorbing them and rebounding stronger than before. Life-changing experiences are not something you can plan for, which is often difficult for businesspeople to accept; executives love to anticipate various scenarios and prepare their responses in advance. Instead, they tend to come out of the blue, when it's too late to prepare. However, you can live your life in a way that allows you to accept setbacks as they occur, move on, and create new possibilities.

Since my injury, I've had the opportunity to explore resilience from my own standpoint as well as through numerous conversations with leaders and others who have been through life-altering events. My hope is that by sharing my story I can show people that they can create a new future after a crisis hits. As for those who are taking on the challenges of everyday life, perhaps they can look to some of the lessons I've learned for insights into how they might prepare for the worst.

Choose to Go Forward

Accepting adversity and moving on isn't easy and can take time. You don't have to like or somehow justify what's happened. You just have to decide that you can live with it. Pretty early on, I decided that I could live without the use of my legs, which was just as well, because I couldn't change the past. Better to focus on things over which I did have some control—for example, how would I move on and live a full life?

Everyone I know who's been through a major crisis can remember the exact moment that he or she chose to accept what had happened and to go forward. People remember where they were, what they were wearing, whom they were with, what the weather was like— every detail. For me, the defining moment came after those first few terribly bleak weeks in the hospital. I was lying in my bed, looking out the window, and I told myself that I still had a lot to offer. Although I was physically limited, my brain still worked. Because I had played various leadership roles before my injury, maybe my future could entail leading by example—that is, demonstrating the ability to bounce back after adversity. I even thought about writing an article about my experience for *Harvard Business Review*. That this particular detail came to pass is not what is important; what matters is that it was a positive and concrete image representing what could be part of my new future, even if I hadn't yet imagined how I would get there.

The primary reason I was able to let go of the past without regrets was that an outpouring of support from family and friends showed me that my old life had already proved to be of value and made a difference. All of us have been there for a family member, a friend, a colleague, or even an acquaintance in a time of need. We touch people's lives, but we don't necessarily realize how much. It's easy to underestimate the impact we have. But people notice and remember. In my first couple of months in the hospital, I received a few hundred cards, more than half of which came from people I had gotten to know through my 20 years of consulting work at CSC Index. The letters were humbling and rewarding. None of them simply expressed regret and support. Everyone wrote paragraphs, recounting our times together and instances of my helping them in some way—simple acts of kindness that became lasting memories for them. I had long forgotten most of these incidents. The letters recalled deeply personal conversations, some of which dated back a decade or more. One person wrote about the time he and I had been stranded together in Minnesota on business while he'd been going through a divorce; he said I had been a source of comfort to him. Another wrote that he would never forget my flying to Chicago to meet him for dinner after he was fired from his job of 20 years.

Reading those letters felt something like being present for my own eulogy. Few people get to "listen in" the way I did. I was moved, of course—but more important, it was liberating knowing that I had made a difference in others' lives and that I no longer had that to prove. And happily, I had the opportunity to bring all those experiences and relationships with me into a new life.

There is no way I could have overcome the trauma and found hope without a caring community. To survive, you need at least one true believer, someone who will have faith in your ability to recover even when you lose it yourself. I was lucky enough to have my children and my wife, whose heroics I won't detail here, because that would be a book in itself. Not everybody has strong family ties, though, and crisis does put a strain on them, particularly if they are tenuous from the start. The letters I received served as a reminder that you can create a caring community in any context, even at work. People will care about you if you authentically care about them.

Seek Perspective

When you undergo a sudden loss, your routine is interrupted, and your mind becomes preoccupied with trying to make sense of what happened. In the early days, I had a lot of time to think, and I pondered the inequities of life, which I had just experienced firsthand. Why did this happen? Why me? What could I have done to prevent this? Whom can I blame?

I was also consumed by questions about the future. Are we going to be able to continue living in our house? Will we be able to send the kids to college? What about my responsibilities at home? Will I be able to work? How much will I be able to earn? At times, my emotions distorted my sense of reality. I briefly imagined myself becoming homeless, forced to sell pencils from a tin cup on the corner.

In the end, I came to realize it's fruitless to wish you could change the past, and it's overwhelming to obsess about the future. I also came to understand that "Why me?" is a natural question but one that can't be answered. Such things can happen to anybody. So I decided to put my energy into the present: getting better. That's where I think my work experience helped me gain perspective, because I had guided executives through some pretty dramatic organizational changes. At times I saw experienced, capable people lose their jobs in the process. I saw what they went through, and I saw them rebound.

During my hospital stay, I was vividly reminded that there are always people who are worse off. I was in a rehabilitation ward with 14 other patients. Four were teenagers. When their parents came to visit, you could see the grief on their faces. One patient was a 17-year-old girl who had lost the use of her arms and legs after a diving accident. I reflected: I'm 52 years old. I've had a great career. I've been married for 20 years to a loving wife, and we have two wonderful children. Why should I feel sorry for myself?

Re-Create Your Identity

A crisis challenges your sense of identity. If you're fired, you question your professional abilities. If a loved one dies, you lose a defining relationship. A physical crisis like mine robs you of some of the basic elements of independence. One of my first tasks in building my new life was reclaiming my dignity and identity.

This is something I struggled with from day one in the hospital. I was so accustomed to my independence that it was hard for me to adjust to needing help from others—I wanted to be able to do things on my own schedule rather than at others' convenience. I certainly didn't want to become an obligation or burden to my family. I had a fleeting and degrading image of myself as the new family pet. ("Who's going to walk the dog? I did it last night; it's your turn.") It was an absurd image, but it was a visceral, emotional reaction to my diminished physical capacity.

Adding to my frustration was overhearing people in white coats conferring about me in low tones as though I were a case study. Truth be told, after an entire career spent analyzing and talking about other people and organizations, I realized I *was* a case study. So I began to assert myself by joining the conversations and putting in my two cents, even contributing ideas about how the hospital could be run better. It was my way of saying, "I'm not just a body. I have a point of view, something to bring to the table."

Despite my optimism and determination, my first experiences in public were difficult. Most people have limited contact with the physically disabled. To some, I stand out—I feel as though a wheelchair puts a spotlight on me. But I can be easily overlooked as well. For one thing, I'm not at eye level with my peers unless they're sitting down. For another, many people have preconceived notions about those of us in wheelchairs that go beyond our physical limitations. I've learned to counterbalance my physical disadvantages by being more outgoing and assertive than I was before. I now initiate conversations all the time. I want to demonstrate that I still have something of value to offer. To this day, my energy sometimes takes others by surprise; it's hard for them to reconcile what they expect with what they see and hear.

The transition was uncomfortable at first. I had come to terms with the fact that I wouldn't be returning to my old life, but I didn't yet know who I was becoming. Still, being in between the two places was freeing. I refused to put limits on myself, even in ways I might have in the past.

The new me is driven and fearless—sometimes I feel invincible. When I see an opportunity to participate, I don't ask for permission; I just jump right in. I say to myself, "What's the worst that could happen? I've already discovered a deep bottom, and I'm OK."

Raise the Bar

I've always had an inclination to aim high. I was one of the first in my family to attend college, which opened doors previously unknown to me. Then, at CSC Index, our consulting practice constantly pushed clients to achieve ever more aggressive goals, and I witnessed some pretty astonishing results. So during my rehabilitation, I decided that I wouldn't compromise my ambitions. Instead, I would raise the bar: If I can survive this injury, what else can I do? My first victory was to survive; now I would find a new way to lead.

When I got out of the hospital, I moved as quickly as I could to reestablish myself as a professional. With 30 years of consulting experience under my belt, I knew I could still contribute something of use. It would have to be on new terms, though; I would have to take into account my physical limitations. About 18 months earlier, I had left my old company and, with a partner, launched a new firm. I'd been largely responsible for marketing, a role that requires a lot of hustle, especially at a start-up. After the injury, I didn't have the stamina to jump right back in, so my partner and I decided to put my involvement in that company on the back burner. What to do instead?

Once again, the network I had developed in my previous life proved invaluable. I made my first significant post-injury public appearance that September, at a reunion of CSC Index alumni. The person hosting the event invited me to say something, and I was happy to do so. The group got extremely quiet, and I asked everybody to sit down—which they did, mostly on the floor. I had a chance to tell everyone there how much their support had meant to me, and because

Wisdom from Adversity

A TRAUMATIC EVENT FORCES YOU to rethink your life and your beliefs. Since my injury, I've spoken with numerous people who have gone through crises, and certain themes have repeatedly come up. Some are truisms that we've known since childhood, but they don't really take root until you face a serious challenge to your identity. Below, I've summarized a few of the lessons I've learned.

You can't know what will happen tomorrow—and it's better that way
If we knew all the good and bad things in store for us, we would probably focus on preventing the bad. It's far more rewarding to engage with the present.

You can't control what happens, just how you respond
Successful people are accustomed to being in control, but adversity strikes unannounced. The only way to influence the outcome is by focusing on the things you have the power to control: the choices you make in response to life's events.

Adversity distorts reality but crystallizes the truth
It reinforces your fears but also puts an emphasis on what matters right now. Adversity also sheds light on your beliefs: It shows you what is important to you, who your friends are, what you are capable of, and what your true goals and ambitions are.

Loss amplifies the value of what remains
It pushes you (and may force you) to take stock of what you have, allowing you to liberate yourself from petty or irrelevant matters and celebrate your assets.

It's easier to create new dreams than to cling to broken ones
Adversity alters relationships and may even ruin them. It destroys some dreams and renders others unlikely. Certain things will be irrevocably lost, and pretending otherwise is foolish. But adversity also provides an opportunity to houseclean—to pack old dreams away and make room for new ones.

Your happiness is more important than righting injustices
Anger is a normal response to a traumatic event, but attempting to assign blame or seek justice is draining and usually futile. It's more fruitful to release the anger and move forward with your life.

they were sitting, I didn't have to look up to see their faces. It was very moving for me.

Nine months after my injury, I held two brainstorming sessions, each including eight or nine people I trusted, with one of them acting as a facilitator. The goal was to help me shape my thinking about what I could do professionally now. We began with the idea that my medical condition could be a platform that would give me access to new people and enhanced credibility in delivering a message about achievement. I didn't want to limit myself to consulting on crisis but hoped to use my experience to help others fulfill their ambitions despite perceived constraints. I also wanted to consider more traditional business opportunities. We came up with a variety of possibilities ranging from advising hospitals on how to help patients reenter the world to coaching executives to raise the level of ambition for themselves and their teams, looking at each idea through the lenses of personal interest and enrichment, feasibility, and income potential.

About six months later, a former colleague called me to join a consulting project he had taken on, helping a group of senior executives launch a firm aimed at the baby boomer demographic. The work was interesting, but what mattered most to me was reengaging in the world of business. A full workday was physically exhausting at first, and just getting there—driving into downtown Boston, finding a place to park, and rolling to the office—was very stressful. But it was exhilarating to be back at work. I told myself, "I can still do this."

Since then, I've discovered many causes to which I can contribute my time and expertise. I developed an interest in the Christopher Reeve Foundation, so I got in touch with its directors. I've now done a few projects with the foundation, most recently acting as the local host of a worldwide summit for its spinal cord researchers. I also testified on behalf of stem cell research at a legislative hearing at the Massachusetts State House—and was surprised to find myself on the news that night and on the front page of the newspaper the next morning. I'm giving back to my community, as well. I sit on the boards of several not-for-profits, and I'm the executive-in-residence at the University of Massachusetts, my alma mater. Not long before my injury, I'd launched an executive breakfast program, a forum for interviewing accomplished alumni. My ties to the university were identified at the early brainstorming sessions as an important asset I should hold on to; I've missed only one breakfast, which was held while I was in the hospital. Today, the breakfast group has grown from 250 members to 1,800 since my injury. The injury has enriched my management consulting practice, too, as I can combine my recent experience with my business background to advise leaders who are facing adversity in their personal lives or at their organizations. In my new life, I am able to use all of my assets, including my paralysis, to be a new kind of leader.

Many of us underestimate our ability to withstand crisis. I certainly did. If you had asked me before my injury how I would handle being paralyzed, I would have said something to the effect of "You might as well put me in a corner and shoot me." I quickly changed my mind about that. Not that I like being in a wheelchair—I struggle every day with the additional limits and challenges that paralysis has imposed upon me.

But rather than feel sorry for myself, I've chosen to use what I accomplished in my previous life as a foundation for building a second life full of purpose and possibilities, some of which only became visible thanks to my injury. My new life's a work in progress, and I have to re-create parts of myself every day. I know that this life is full of new adventures, though, even if I don't know what all of them are yet. I may experience them sitting down, but in a way I am standing taller than ever.

Originally published in March 2007. Reprint R0703J

Extreme Negotiations

by Jeff Weiss, Aram Donigian, and Jonathan Hughes

IT'S OFTEN NOT EASY TO "GET TO YES," particularly given the pace of business and the structure of organizations today. CEOs and other senior executives are under extreme time pressure, managing complex, high-stakes conversations across functional areas and divisions, with alliance partners and critical suppliers, and with customers and regulators. Many report feeling that they are constantly in negotiation mode—trying to gain approval for deals in which hundreds of millions (and sometimes billions) of dollars are at stake, in the shortest possible time frames, from people who may hold the company's (and even the leader's own) future in their hands. To these executives, negotiation isn't just about transactions anymore; it's about adapting to rapidly changing information and circumstances.

U.S. military officers around the globe confront this sort of challenge every day—patrolling in hot spots like Afghanistan and Iraq, attempting to persuade wary local leaders to share valuable information while simultaneously trying to distinguish friend from foe, balancing the need to protect their troops with the need to build indigenous support for America's regional and global interests.

The business and military contexts are quite different, but leaders in both face negotiations in which the traps are many and good advice is scarce. We call these "dangerous negotiations"—meaning not that they are necessarily aimed at solving an immediate life-and-death crisis but that the stakes involved put intense pressure on a leader.

Clearly, the danger for a business leader who is trying to reach an agreement with a single-source supplier, close a multibillion-dollar deal with a target company before its stock dives any further, or renegotiate prices with a dissatisfied customer differs from that for a soldier negotiating with villagers for intelligence on the source of rocket attacks. But the perception of danger prompts business and military leaders to resort to the same kinds of behavior. Both commonly feel pressure to make rapid progress, project strength and control (especially when they have neither), rely on coercion rather than collaboration, trade resources for cooperation rather than get genuine buy-in, and offer unilateral concessions to mitigate possible threats.

U.S. military officers serving in Afghanistan have found themselves trying to hold these pressures at bay while engaging, often daily, in dangerous negotiations. Over the past six years or so, we've studied how they resolve conflict and influence others in situations where the levels of risk and uncertainty are off the charts. We find that the most skilled among them rely on five highly effective strategies: (1) understand the big picture, (2) uncover hidden agendas and collaborate with the other side, (3) get genuine buy-in, (4) build relationships that are based on trust rather than fear, and (5) pay attention to process as well as desired outcomes. These strategies, used in combination, are characteristic of effective *in extremis* negotiators, to adapt a term from Colonel Thomas Kolditz, a professor at the U.S. Military Academy at West Point and the author of *In Extremis Leadership.*

Negotiation behaviors tend to be deeply ingrained and are often reactive rather than deliberate, especially in dangerous situations. These five strategies can help business negotiators not only to respond quickly at the bargaining table but also to reshape their thinking *ahead* of the deal. Let's take a closer look at each of them and how they've been implemented by officers in Afghanistan.

Strategy 1: Get the Big Picture

Start by soliciting the other person's or group's point of view. Use what you learn to shape the objectives of the negotiation and to determine how you'll achieve them.

Idea in Brief

Business leaders today report feeling that they must constantly negotiate to extract complex agreements from people with power over industries or individual careers. Sensing that they're in continual danger makes them want to act fast, project control (even when they don't have any), rely on coercion, and defuse tension at any cost.

The end result may be a compromise that fails to address the real problem or opportunity, increased resistance from the other side that makes agreement impossible, resentment that sours future negotiations, a failure to develop relationships based on mutual respect and trust, or an agreement that creates enormous exposure to future risk.

To avoid these dangers, executives can apply the same strategies used by well-trained military officers in hot spots like Afghanistan and Iraq. Those *in extremis* negotiators solicit others' points of view, propose multiple solutions and invite their counterparts to critique them, use facts and principles of fairness to persuade the other side, systematically build trust and commitments over time, and take steps to reshape the negotiation process as well as the outcome.

Negotiators in dangerous situations try to act fast to reduce the perceived level of threat. They often dive into discussions before they've fully assessed the situation, reacting to assumptions and gut feelings—and they tend not to test or revisit those assumptions. So business and military leaders alike end up negotiating on the basis of incomplete or incorrect information—which often leads to conflict, impasse, or a solution that addresses only part of the problem or opportunity. But in fact they usually have more time than they realize to talk, consider, and respond.

When Taliban fighters set fire to an Afghan supply truck less than two miles from his combat outpost, Sergeant First Class Michael Himmel (his and all other officers' names have been changed, as have the locations in which the incidents described in this article occurred) knew that an immediate response was required. But all U.S. units were on patrol, so he decided this was a good opportunity for the Afghan National Police to handle a crisis situation on their own. (Himmel's platoon had been training and patrolling with the ANP for six months.) The ANP chief, a 55-year-old local man with 30 years of police experience, immediately pushed back. He tried to express his concern about performing a solo mission and requested support. "My men are inadequately prepared," he said—indirectly blaming Himmel for this state of affairs. The sergeant, who was locked into the assumptions he'd made about the chief and his team, ignored the request and insisted that all they lacked was "courage and a commitment to hard work." The chief of course felt disrespected. Eventually he sent a poorly equipped team to investigate the fire. Not surprisingly, the men came back with little information.

First Lieutenant Daniel Dubay handled a similar negotiation much differently. While on patrol near the village of Azrow, Dubay's platoon came under attack from two buildings about 200 yards away. After 45 minutes of fighting, the anticoalition forces disappeared into nearby *qalats* (fortified shelters). The platoon went into assessment mode, checking for injuries among the citizens. Dubay and a squad moved to the building that most of the shots had come from. They discovered 25 women and children huddled in a small room. Without entering the room, Dubay explained through an interpreter that his platoon had just been fired on and he was looking for information that might help identify the insurgents who had been in the compound.

"There are no bad guys here—no one was firing at you," one woman barked, her voice shaking a bit.

Dubay needed information fast. He could have obeyed his instincts and started making harsh demands. But he recognized the women's fear—and his own—and decided to slow things down, test his assumption that the women were collaborating with the enemy, and change his approach to getting the intelligence he needed.

He took off his dark glasses, slung his weapon onto his back, and knelt just outside the room. He reassured the women that their homes were now secured by both Afghan and American forces and said he just wanted to understand why they were all clustered in this one room. Over the next 15 or 20 minutes he talked softly, acknowledging their fright at being caught in the middle of a firefight. Finally, one woman came forward and spoke about the men who had herded them all into this room and then taken up positions. Dubay thanked her. Another

Implementing Strategy 1: Get the Big Picture

Avoid

- Assuming you have all the facts: "Look, it's obvious that . . ."
- Assuming the other side is biased—but you're not
- Assuming the other side's motivations and intentions are obvious—and probably nefarious

Instead

- Be curious: "Help me understand how you see the situation."
- Be humble: "What do I have wrong?"
- Be open-minded: "Is there another way to explain this?"

---

woman spoke up. The men were not Afghan, she said; they looked like foreign fighters. Three or four other women offered more details.

Dubay took notes and amended his objective: He would not only gather the information he needed about this particular situation but also develop an ongoing relationship with these women to get information in the future. He gave them a card providing the phone number of the district center; promised to check in on them two days later, when his platoon would be on patrol in that village again; and asked that they share information with him as they discovered it. He established mutual respect with the people of Azrow—a relationship that paid off in the months that followed.

Strategy 2: Uncover and Collaborate

Learn the other party's motivations and concerns. Propose multiple solutions and invite your counterparts to improve on them.

As well as pressuring people to act fast, a threatening situation makes them want to look strong and more in control than they probably are. In this state of mind, negotiators tend to stake out extreme positions and make aggressive demands. Unfortunately, that almost always triggers or exacerbates resistance from the other side.

Discussions become contentious and inefficient, and both parties run the risk of a stalemate.

Captain Chris Caldwell received intelligence that the soldiers in his company had inflicted casualties on the enemy. He knew there was only one Afghan medical center in the area equipped to treat the wounded. Seeking to assert his company's control in the region, Caldwell went to the center to interview a doctor who was known to be a Taliban sympathizer. After being denied permission to enter, Caldwell forced his way into the facility, found evidence that the enemy combatants were being treated, and detained the doctor for questioning.

When they heard about Caldwell's actions, the village elders paid an angry visit to the captain. He defended himself, stating that he would respond differently in the future only if the locals began working with, not against, his troops. The elders argued in turn that the villagers would cooperate only when they were given an incentive—that is, when they were shown respect. One such sign, they said, would be a big boost in reconstruction dollars. Caldwell told them that if they wanted anything from him, they would have to give him information about the wounded people at the clinic. This enraged the elders, and the negotiation spiraled out of control.

The skilled *in extremis* negotiator focuses on turning negotiation into side-by-side problem solving rather than a test of wills. Captain Andrew Williams, an artillery battery commander in Ghazni, received a report that his soldiers had seen an improvised explosive device being placed along a roadside. He instructed them not to use force but to monitor the site and identify the men who were planting IEDs. (His team would eventually remove and detonate the devices in a controlled environment.) Once he had this information in hand, Williams went to the village where the men lived, gathered the elders, and told them he wanted IED placements in the area to stop. The elders said that as long as they received money in return, they would make sure the villagers complied.

Given the time and safety pressures he was feeling, Williams was tempted to ask, "How much?" Instead he asked, "Why?" He explained that he couldn't offer the elders anything unless he understood what

Implementing Strategy 2:
Uncover and Collaborate

Avoid

- Making open-ended offers: "What do you want?"
- Making unilateral offers: "I'd be willing to . . ."
- Simply agreeing to (or refusing) the other side's demands

Instead

- Ask "Why is that important to you?"
- Propose solutions for critique: "Here's a possibility—what might be wrong with it?"

---

they were trying to achieve. Eventually they told him they would need to pay for information about who was responsible for planting IEDs—and money was obviously in short supply. They also wanted to give some of the money to the village, to preserve their status and prove that they weren't just informants.

Williams made a reasoned counteroffer: His men would do the work of identifying the culprits, and the elders would be responsible for taking them to the nearest American combat outpost. Seeking to draw the elders out and engage them as partners, he asked, "What would be wrong with this idea?"

Surprisingly, the elders liked the plan but expressed concern that the captured men were not extremists, just short on cash and trying to support their families. Williams said that if the elders took the men to the combat outpost and let the Americans enter their names into a database, then they could take the men back to the village. He added that this would help them build prestige with the villagers, because they'd be handling the situation themselves. The elders agreed. Two days later they arrived with the wanted men, whose names were entered into the database. The men were warned about future actions and allowed to return to the village and their families.

Before long, record numbers of weapons caches were being turned in, and locals were warning soldiers on patrol about IEDs that lay ahead and voluntarily reporting information on mortar launch sites.

Strategy 3: Elicit Genuine Buy-In

Use facts and the principles of fairness, rather than brute force, to persuade others. Arm them with ways to defend their decisions to their critics, and create useful precedents for future negotiations.

Danger often tempts negotiators to play hardball, using coercion to make deals. That typically engenders resentment and leads to future conflict, making follow-on negotiations much more difficult. Of course, a hostile takeover isn't quite the same as an armed standoff. But the terms presented can be similarly stark or shocking.

Captain Kyle Lauers's first mission in Afghanistan was simple on its face: Capture or kill Wahid Salat, a Taliban leader who was staying in a nearby village. But he felt tremendous pressure to get his 130 soldiers in and out safely. The main challenge would be negotiating with the local police chief and the village elder for help in securing the building where Salat was staying. When Lauers asked the police chief to apprehend Salat, the chief flatly refused.

"We need to move now," Lauers told the chief. "If you won't help, I can't be responsible for what happens." The chief said nothing. Lauers ordered his platoon to cordon off the building. As shots rang out, he spotted the village elder approaching from across the street, clearly angry and confused. The elder began to shout at Lauers just as the platoon leader reported over the radio that the suspect and three bodyguards had been killed. The elder demanded to know why Lauers's company had entered the village and started shooting without any ANP support or discussions with the elder. Lauers explained that the police chief had refused to cooperate. The elder immediately turned the blame back on Lauers and demanded money for damages. Lauers replied that since the Taliban were responsible for the damages, the elder could get reparation from *them*. He then left to check on his men.

Over the next 11 months this village continued to be a problem for Lauers's company. Regular mortar attacks were staged from the vicinity. Whenever officers wanted information from anyone in the village, they had to pay in either money or supplies—and even then they were often given the wrong names, places, or dates. Threats and force have their place, especially in certain military situations. In this case, however, Lauers's negotiation strategy compromised both his near and his long-term objectives.

The effective *in extremis* negotiator recognizes that his objectives will almost always be better achieved if he elicits true buy-in rather than grudging compliance from the other side. Upon his arrival in Afghanistan, Captain John Chang found that his company's Afghan National Army counterparts were regularly using threats, especially in dangerous or high-stakes contexts, to change the local population's behavior. Chang knew enough about both Afghan culture and the Koran to understand the value the locals put on respectful treatment. He decided that if he could change the way his soldiers interacted with the ANA, he could affect how the ANA worked with the villagers. He invited ANA soldiers to move into the Americans' combat outpost. The two units began to eat, train, plan, patrol, and relax together, resulting in a true partnership. Within a month the ANA was serving as an advocate for the U.S.-led mission, explaining to village elders that the Americans were guests in their country—operating to help people at the request of the Afghan government—and reminding them of the cultural importance of hospitality in Afghanistan.

When violence later erupted in the area, a precedent had been set. Rather than make threats, Captain Chang and his ANA counterpart solicited recommendations from the village elders about how to provide better security in the valley and asked what justifications the elders would need to defend any pacts the U.S. and ANA forces made. The elders voiced their objections to coalition forces' searching homes, detaining people in the middle of the night, and randomly stopping and searching vehicles. They talked about being afraid to hunt or to let livestock graze in the mountains, where U.S.

Implementing Strategy 3: Elicit Genuine Buy-In

Avoid

- Threats: "You'd better agree, or else . . ."
- Arbitrariness: "I want it because I want it."
- Close-mindedness: "Under no circumstances will I agree to—or even consider—that proposal."

Instead

- Appeal to fairness: "What *should* we do?"
- Appeal to logic and legitimacy: "I think this makes sense, because . . ."
- Consider constituent perspectives: "How can each of us explain this agreement to colleagues?"

---

forces were shooting artillery. Any negotiated agreement about reducing the violence, they advised, would have to show respect for personal liberties and local laws. Most important, it should look like an ANA—not a U.S.—solution. Chang and his ANA counterpart crafted an agreement that the elders could defend to the populace, and Taliban recruitment in the area dropped significantly.

Strategy 4: Build Trust First

Deal with relationship issues head-on. Make incremental commitments to encourage trust and cooperation.

When stakes and risks are at their highest, business and military leaders are often tempted to take the quick and easy path of trading resources for help. After all, a dangerous situation doesn't provide the time to develop a good working relationship or to fix whatever stands in the way of one. But making substantive concessions almost always invites extortion and breeds disrespect or outright contempt.

Military officers frequently fall prey to the concession trap. Farrukh, an Afghan, had opened a girls' school outside Baraki and was continually harassed by local Taliban leaders. Intelligence officers discovered that a known insurgent had made a call to Farrukh's cell phone. They seized the phone and found that Farrukh had received calls from several other Taliban leaders. They arrested him, and Farrukh served 12 months in a detention center, waiting for a hearing. Eventually he got his time in court and was found not guilty. But in the meantime, his school had been closed, his reputation had been severely damaged, and he had suffered considerable physical hardship. He had to be compensated.

The Army officer in charge offered a sum of money for lost wages. Farrukh wanted more: an explanation for his arrest and detention, and procedures that could be put in place to avoid such misunderstandings in the future. The officer simply threw in an additional sum for his pain and suffering and sent him on his way, barely offering an apology. Farrukh—who was a leader in his village and had a long history of working with Western peacekeeping forces—left with $12,000 in his pocket, but he vowed never to trust an American again. Worse yet, as he told his story to others, their distrust grew, making it difficult for U.S. officers to get any sort of useful intelligence or active cooperation from the villagers.

Skilled *in extremis* negotiators never make arbitrary concessions in an effort to buy goodwill. Instead they build trust over time through incremental and reciprocal commitments. Captain Aaron Davis was deployed to Khost Province with orders to settle "quickly and finally" several long-standing disputes with local leaders. Within a week of his arrival Davis headed out to a village where a man named Haji Said Ullah owned what had once been a lucrative gas station. Ullah's business had all but dried up two years earlier, when U.S. forces closed a road to secure a newly built airfield, preventing people from getting to his pump. For two years, various Army officers had promised Ullah both compensation and aid in finding his brother, who he suspected had been kidnapped by Taliban forces. None of their promises had been kept. No wonder, then, that Ullah greeted Davis with disdain—and a demand for more money. Davis resisted the temptation to throw cash at the problem; this was, at its core, a relationship issue.

Implementing Strategy 4: Build Trust First

Avoid

- Trying to "buy" a good relationship
- Offering concessions to repair breaches of trust, whether actual or only perceived

Instead

- Explore how a breakdown in trust may have occurred and how to remedy it.
- Make concessions only if they are a legitimate way to compensate for losses owing to your nonperformance or broken commitments.
- Treat counterparts with respect, and act in ways that will command theirs.

Davis visited Ullah several times, listening to his angry tales and asking questions. At no point did he offer compensation. He did, however, tell Ullah that he would look into what had happened and return within three days. The two men sat down for tea three days later, and the captain offered apologies for what Ullah had been through and updates on what he had learned. He asked for Ullah's help in figuring out how to repair the relationship and, ultimately, rebuild trust with other local leaders. The men talked about ways to get information concerning Ullah's brother, how to improve communication between U.S. forces and villagers, and how to make the population more secure. Only then did Davis turn back to the question of compensation, sharing his estimate of Ullah's business losses as judged by local standards. (It was a basic calculation, but no one else had bothered to do it.) Ullah considered the numbers and within a few minutes agreed to what he deemed a fair figure—a small fraction of what he'd initially demanded.

Training Officers to Negotiate

Why do military officers need to negotiate?

For those in Iraq and Afghanistan, the nature of the job has changed. In a 2005 briefing at West Point, one division commander outlined a day in Baghdad for his lieutenants: going on patrol at 0700, helping set up a local market at 0900, working to restore power to a city block at 1200, attending a town council meeting at 1800, and conducting a raid on a suspected insurgent's residence at 0100. Each of these missions involved some type of negotiation.

Why don't demands and threats work just as well?

Sometimes they do; and sometimes they are necessary. But these officers face increasingly complex situations involving multiple parties, issues, and cultures. The stakes can be life and death, physical security, critical scarce resources, or political capital. In July 2010 General David Petraeus reminded our forces in Afghanistan to focus on the decisive human element. That keeps military leaders at all levels mentally agile and adaptable—not just skilled with weapons and combat protocol.

How do you train *in extremis* negotiators?

At West Point we focus on applied practice. For instance, the course Negotiation for Leaders presents case studies for discussion. Each class introduces a bargaining strategy applicable to the case at hand. We systematically review the approach cadets took to each case study—looking hard at how and why they made the choices they did.

We also do one-on-one coaching to help officers examine their own tactics, using probing questions such as: How did you react when your counterpart made a threat? Why did you react that way—what was your goal? What response did you expect? Given the outcome, would you change your approach in the future? If so, how and why?

Interactions with superiors provide further learning. If a commander asks a negotiating officer if he got the other side to back down or if he kept it "happy," the officer probably won't develop the strategic thought process and skills *in extremis* negotiators need. But if the commander asks how well the officer understood and addressed the other side's concerns and motivations, or whether the outcome sets a good and easily explained precedent for others, the officer is likely to begin thinking strategically about negotiations.

Business executives, too, can use these methods to develop the negotiating skills of their organizations' leaders.

Strategy 5: Focus on Process

Consciously change the game by not reacting to the other side. Take steps to shape the negotiation process as well as the outcome.

In negotiations that they perceive to be dangerous, executives and officers naturally want to avoid harm to themselves or their constituents. Together with the inevitable need to act quickly, that creates pressure for them to give in on critical issues—not a good idea. The resulting agreement may create an exposure to risk far beyond the immediate threat.

First Lieutenant Matthew Frye and his platoon had been under rocket attack for eight straight days, at about the same time each day, at the forward operating base where they were stationed. On the ninth day, while his platoon was patrolling, Frye received word that insurgents were preparing another attack on the base and that his group should investigate the vicinity where earlier attacks had originated. He felt intense pressure to quickly determine the current location, description, and disposition of the enemy. After all, one of the last rockets launched had landed only about 400 yards from his tent.

Once in the vicinity, Frye sought information from the elders and asked what they wanted in exchange for giving him the insurgents' names. Not surprisingly, they requested a great deal—primarily in the form of food, water, and clothing. Frye promised to provide this humanitarian assistance, but when he asked for information in return, the elders denied knowing anything about the insurgents. Wanting to protect his men, Frye made further offers: emergency relief funds and assistance from his soldiers on a well project. The elders accepted but again were mum. Realizing that he was being taken, Frye said his promises had been contingent on receiving information. The elders were angry that he was backing away from his commitments and suggested that Frye and his men should be extra careful when they headed back to their base.

Feeling threatened and nervous, Frye agreed to fulfill the one-sided bargain and said he hoped the elders would be a little more cooperative the next time. He came away with neither the information he needed nor a good working relationship with the elders. Intelligence later confirmed that the enemy had watched the Americans throughout their visit to the village—so he had created even more danger for his platoon.

Frye's first mistake, of course, was believing that he had only two options: to refuse the elders' demands, in which case he and his men would remain in danger, or to simply capitulate and hope for the best. He should have stepped back from the issues immediately at hand, analyzed the elders' tactics, and considered how to shape the negotiation process to his advantage.

On his first patrol in Kunduz, First Lieutenant Billy Gardner was leading his platoon through a bazaar when he was approached by five men. The men, who represented apple farmers in the local agricultural cooperative, were angry that a previous American unit had given the district several million dollars to purchase land for the expansion of its forward operating base. The person the district subgovernor had paid was not the legal landowner, and the men demanded that they and their fellow farmers be compensated immediately. A crowd gathered, the men began making threats, and when Gardner did not respond, they demanded even more in compensation. They tried to involve Gardner's squad members in the negotiation, angrily directing some of their demands to one while being extremely solicitous of another.

Gardner recognized their divide-and-conquer ploy. He refused to respond to it, and he refused to compromise. If he did either, he would be rewarding negotiating behaviors that he wanted no part of. Instead, Gardner set about changing the nature of the conversation. He sat down, greeted the men in Pashto, took off his helmet, put down his rifle, and listened attentively. He spoke slowly and quietly. In no time, the farmers' body language changed and their shouting diminished. In fact, they were straining to hear Gardner. He began asking questions in a manner that was both respectful (he didn't insist on his point of view) and commanding. He assumed the natural demeanor of a judge—one seeking to impartially determine the appropriate course of action and having the authority to do so.

Implementing Strategy 5:
Focus on Process

Avoid

- Acting without gauging how your actions will be perceived and what the response will be
- Ignoring the consequences of a given action for future as well as current negotiations

Instead

- Talk not just about the issues but about the negotiation process: "We seem to be at an impasse; perhaps we should spend some more time exploring our respective objectives and constraints."
- Slow down the pace: "I'm not ready to agree, but I'd prefer not to walk away either. I think this warrants further exploration."
- Issue warnings without making threats: "Unless you're willing to work with me toward a mutually acceptable outcome, I can't afford to spend more time negotiating."

Gardner asked the men about the nature of their business arrangements, their crops, whom they represented, and how the land sale had directly affected them. Apples were the mainstay of the local economy, he learned. The men were not opposed to selling the land, but they wanted to be recognized as the lawful owners of the parcels in question. Gardner began to propose some possible solutions. Had they approached the provincial subgovernor about their grievance? he asked. Or taken it to the subdistrict *shura* (council)? They said they had not: They didn't trust the subgovernor, and they thought the shura was ineffective.

Gardner listened without definitively answering when new demands—by now framed as requests for assistance—were put forth. He began to recognize that the cooperative represented a form of stable civil government; here was an opportunity to strengthen democratic practices and institutions. Gardner explained to the men that once the issues had formally been brought to the subgovernor, the Americans would be better able to help. The farmers ultimately agreed to try what he suggested—especially if he would continue to provide them with advice, which he agreed to do. What had begun as an impromptu, tense situation characterized by aggressive behavior evolved into hours of talking, an invitation to stay for lunch, and a conversation that eventually shifted to the farmers' sharing what they knew about recent insurgent activity in the area.

Perhaps the most important lesson the *in extremis* negotiator has to teach both executives and military officers is that in the very context where one feels the most pressure to act fast and stake out an unwavering position, it is best to do neither. Control and power can be asserted most effectively by slowing down the pace of the negotiation, actively leading counterparts into a constructive dialogue, and demonstrating genuine openness to others' perspectives. That isn't giving in. It is being strategic rather than reactive. It's thinking several moves ahead about how your actions might be perceived. And it's making tactical choices that elicit constructive responses and advance your true objectives.

Originally published in November 2010. Reprint R1011C

Post-Traumatic Growth and Building Resilience

An interview with Martin E.P. Seligman
by Sarah Green Carmichael

Sarah Green: Welcome to the HBR IdeaCast from *Harvard Business Review*, I'm Sarah Green. I'm talking today with University of Pennsylvania Professor Martin Seligman, the man known as the father of positive psychology. He's the author of the new book, *Flourish*, and of the HBR article, "Building Resilience" in the April 2011 issue of the magazine. Marty, thanks so much for talking with us today.

Martin Seligman: Glad to be here.

Sarah Green: I know it's a huge project, but I'd like to start with having you just give us a quick encapsulation of the work that you've been doing with the United States Army, which is the foundation of the article.

Martin Seligman: About two and a half years ago, the chief of staff of the army called me to the Pentagon and said, suicide, post-traumatic stress disorder, substance abuse, divorce, depression. What does positive psychology say about that, Dr. Seligman? And there was a meeting with general staff and I said that the human reaction to extreme adversity—combat, being laid off, divorce—is bell-shaped. And on the left-hand side, you got people who fall apart. And those are five ways in which we fall apart: anxiety, depression, suicide, post-traumatic stress disorder. And I thought the Army should continue to spend $5 to $10 billion a year treating those things. But the Army is not a hospital. And there are two really important things about the reaction to adversity.

The majority of people are resilient. And what that means is they go through a tough time after unemployment, after rejection, after combat, but a month or two later, by our psychological and physical measures, they're back where they were. And then a large number of people show what's called post-traumatic growth. And what that means is they typically go through a very hard time, often post-traumatic stress disorder. But a year later they're stronger than they were before by psychological and physical measures. These are the people of whom Nietzsche said, if it doesn't kill me, it makes me stronger. So my recommendation to General Casey was to measure and build resilience, and to create an army, which was what he wanted to do, that was just as psychologically fit as physically fit.

Sarah Green: Well, before we get into some of the how of how that happened, as I was reading the article I realized just how much we, in the media, focus on post-traumatic stress disorder. And I always come away from those articles feeling as if the only way to avoid PTSD is to avoid trauma. Which of course is impossible no matter who you are. I think you actually do us a great service by switching the focus to post-traumatic growth. But I wanted to ask you before we get more into that, do you think that there is a negative impact on people of focusing so much on post-traumatic stress disorder?

Martin Seligman: You've hit on a reality, Sarah. We went up to West Point, and we asked, how many of you are aware of post-traumatic stress disorder? And 97%. And how many of you are aware of post-traumatic growth? It was about 10%. And the reason that's very important is that it's self-fulfilling in the following way. So it just isn't depression. If the only thing you know about is post-traumatic stress disorder and you have some awful event, and the next day you burst into tears, you're going to think, I'm going under. I've got post-dramatic stress disorder. And what that does is worsen the symptoms, which are symptoms of anxiety and depression. Which in turn, makes you think even more certainly that you're going under, which worsens the symptoms.

If, on the other hand, you have just a little bit of medical literacy and you know that crying and mourning and feeling very down are typical, normal reactions to being fired, to combat, and that the usual response is resilience and sometimes growth, that stops the downward spiral. So it's very important for people to know that the normal response to very bad things is not going under. It's not post-traumatic stress disorder. It's resilience and, not infrequently, growth.

Sarah Green: Let's talk a little bit more about some of the characteristics of post-traumatic growth. One of the things you mention in the article is that a key part of it is seeing the failure or the trauma as a fork in the road. What do you mean by that, and why is that so important?

Martin Seligman: Well, very often, extremely bad events lead to personal and moral dilemmas. And they're existential crises in which you have to make decisions. And therefore, we talk about it as a fork in the road. One of the most interesting things about depression, which is the big, big component of post-traumatic stress disorder, it is an emotion that tells you to detach from goals you had. That they're unreachable. And that creates a fork in the road. It makes you ask the question, what other things might I do? What doors might open for me?

And one of the important things about knowing about post-traumatic growth and resilience is when those doors open for you, if you are paralyzed by the depression, by the anxiety, by the symptoms of post-traumatic growth, you're not going to walk through those doors. You're not going to take advantage of them. But knowing that, typically people who suffer very bad events have new doors open for them and that it's important to be prepared to walk through them.

Sarah Green: One of the other key elements that you talk about when you talk about growth after a traumatic event, any event, is the importance of articulating life principles. Why is it so important to do that as sort of the final step in growth?

Martin Seligman: Human beings are ineluctably creatures of narrative, creatures who make meaning, tell stories about their lives. And to the extent you can create a narrative of your trauma, a narrative of unemployment, a narrative of combat in which new principles, a more mature way of viewing the world, arise and you can go, like Orpheus, come back from the underground and make sense of what's in the underground, and tell the world what's in the underground, that there's reason to think that's an important enabling condition after trauma.

Sarah Green: So I'd like to transition now into the sort of nuts and bolts of how you adapted all this information about growth and trauma into a program that would work for the U.S. military.

Martin Seligman: Well, starting about almost 20 years ago, after I had worked on learned helplessness, we began to ask the question, what can you do with human beings to create the opposite of learned helplessness in the face of trauma? So we developed a resilience program called the Penn Resilience Program. And we started to go to schools, first to classrooms, and then to whole schools. And now to national school systems, and we taught a set of skills to teachers. And the teachers then taught them to the students. And we measured the anxiety and depression in students.

So what we had basically found in 21 replications across the world of giving the Penn Resilience Program to teachers to teach was that over the next couple of years, the students of these teachers compared to controls had lower depression and anxiety. So that was the background of our work with the Army. And the next step was again, going back to this meeting with General Casey. When I recommended that the Army try to move the entire distribution toward growth and resilience he said, well, we've read your papers on positive education and we see that you teach teachers these skills and then the teachers teach the students. Well that, Dr. Seligman, is the Army model. And I said, it is? And he said, yeah. We have 40,000 teachers in the Army—the drill sergeants. And so he said, the job should be to train all 40,000 drill sergeants in these skills. They will then teach the entire 1.1-million-person army these skills, and we will measure, very carefully, if that prevents post-traumatic stress disorder. And most importantly, the military isn't a hospital, increases performance, increases what readers of *Harvard Business Review* would call productivity. And so that's what we're in the middle of right now.

Sarah Green: So I know this is still in progress, but can you give us a sense of how it's going?

Martin Seligman: I can give you a subjective sense, but I can't tell you the results. Not because I don't know them, but because Congress has not yet been briefed on them. So in a couple of months I think this will be front-page news. But for now I can tell you what the reaction of the—we've now graduated 3,100 drill sergeants from Penn. And the way that's structured is every month 180 noncommissioned officers come to Penn and we give them 10 days of training in the Penn Resilience Program. It has three parts.

The first part is mental toughness. The second part is leading with strengths. And the third part is new social skills for leadership. And the 10 days are divided. First they learn how to use these skills in their own lives, and then they learn how to teach them. And the results are really fascinating. You can actually watch the results in action from the back of the room.

So on the first day these drill sergeants who are really tough people going through three tours of Iraq and Afghanistan, they're war heroes, and they're very critical as you'd imagine. So many of them, on the first couple of hours, are sitting there leaning back in their chairs. And then by the end of the first day, they're leaning forward and actively participating. We had worried that they would say, girly, touchy-feely psycho babble. And to our astonishment, what we find after 10 days is that the average rating of the program is 4.9 out of 5. Hundreds of them have said, this is the best training I ever had in the Army.

And emblematic is one sergeant who came up to me the day after we had taught active constructive responding to good events and he said, "Last night on the phone my 11-year-old son and I were talking about what he did in Little League that day. He had done something good. And after five minutes my son said, 'Is this really you, Daddy?'" So the results have been to the observer, subjectively, unexpectedly, some would say astonishingly positive. And in the next couple of months, the Pentagon will start publishing the results. And I'm not free to release them at this point.

Sarah Green: Well, it does sound tremendously encouraging, and I can just hear the wheels in my listeners' heads turning saying, OK, it worked for teachers. It worked for drill sergeants. I've got to get my managers to do this. Can you talk a little bit about the challenges you faced in adapting this program from one organizational context to another?

Martin Seligman: It's actually pretty straightforward. So I should say how the Penn Resilience Program came about. We first began it with normal adolescents, with divorced couples. And then we actually adapted it for corporations. So we created a generic model of one, mental toughness, two, leading with strengths, and three, social skills and leadership. So we had a generic model that the Penn Resilience Program used in many settings. Mostly educational, but a bit corporately. And then when the army came along, we adapted the generic model to the military.

Strangely enough, we thought we were going to have to radically change the 10-day program since it wasn't at all military. And then when we started to interview soldiers, what we found was that these were 20-year-olds for the most part. They have cellphones. And when you see post-traumatic stress disorder and rejection, it's not about your buddy being killed. What it is typically, is a rejection back in Kansas City. If you've got a cellphone and before you go into combat, you get into a fight with your wife about the kids' grades and it's the rich or that she's running around with someone. And so we found that most of the examples that we use in schools for teachers, in corporate life, for couples, for depression and adolescence, did pretty well. So we basically changed about 20 to 25% of the content. So that's a long-winded way of saying, Sarah, that this is a readily adaptable program that has been used in a variety of settings and only needs a bit of tinkering with for corporate life.

Sarah Green: That was University of Pennsylvania's Martin Seligman. The book is *Flourish*, and the article, "Building Resilience," appears in the April issue of HBR. For more, go to hbr.org.

Originally aired in March 2011.

About the Contributors

RON ASHKENAS is a senior partner of Schaffer Consulting in Stamford, Connecticut.

WARREN G. BENNIS is a Distinguished Professor of Management at the University of Southern California and the author of the forthcoming book *Still Surprised: A Memoir of a Life in Leadership*, with Patricia Ward Biederman (Jossey-Bass).

ALIA CRUM is an assistant professor of psychology at Stanford University. Her research focuses on how changes in subjective mind-sets can improve health and performance through behavioral, psychological, and physiological mechanisms.

THOMAS CRUM is an author, seminar leader, and performance coach. He works to help individuals and organizations turn conflict into powerful relationships, stress into vitality, and pressure into optimal performance.

ARAM DONIGIAN (aram.donigian@usma.edu), a major in the U.S. Army, is an assistant professor at West Point, where he codirects the Negotiation Project.

RODERICK GILKEY is a professor at the Emory School of Medicine and Goizueta Business School.

JONATHAN HUGHES (jhughes@vantagepartners.com) is a partner at Vantage Partners, specializing in supply chain management, strategic alliances, and change management.

GRAHAM JONES, PhD, has consulted to top performers in business, athletics, and the military for more than 20 years. He was Professor of Elite Performance Psychology at the University of Wales, Bangor. His most recent book is *Thrive On Pressure: Lead and Succeed When Times Get Tough* (McGraw-Hill, 2010). He is currently the managing director of Top Performance Consulting Ltd., based in Wokingham in the UK.

CLINT KILTS is the Dr. Paul Janssen Professor in the department of psychiatry and behavioral sciences.

JIM LOEHR, a performance psychologist, has worked with hundreds of professional athletes, including Monica Seles, Dan Jansen, and Mark O'Meara. Loehr is also a cofounder and the CEO of LGE Performance Systems in Orlando, Florida, a consulting firm that applies training principles developed in sports to business executives. He can be reached at jloehr@lgeperformance.com.

GLENN E. MANGURIAN (gmangurian@frontierworks.com) is a cofounder of FrontierWorks, a management-consulting firm based in Hingham, Massachusetts. He was previously senior vice president at CSC Index in Cambridge, Massachusetts.

JOSHUA D. MARGOLIS is a professor of business administration and the faculty chair of the Christensen Center for Teaching and Learning at Harvard Business School.

MITCHELL LEE MARKS is a leadership professor at San Francisco State University's College of Business and the president of JoiningForces .org.

PHILIP MIRVIS is an organizational psychologist and consultant.

TONY SCHWARTZ is the president and CEO of The Energy Project and the author of *Be Excellent at Anything*. Become a fan of The Energy Project on Facebook and connect with Tony at Twitter.com/ TonySchwartz and Twitter.com/Energy_Project.

MARTIN E.P. SELIGMAN is the Zellerbach Family Professor of Psychology and director of the Positive Psychology Center at the University of Pennsylvania. His latest book is *Flourish: A Visionary New Understanding of Happiness and Well-Being* (Free Press, 2011), from which this article is adapted.

PAUL G. STOLTZ is CEO of PEAK Learning, Inc., Chairman of the Global Resilience Institute, and the originator of the Adversity Quotient (AQ) theory and method, currently used within Harvard Business School's Executive Education program.

ROBERT J. THOMAS is a managing director of Accenture Strategy. He is the author of eight books on leadership and organizational change, including *Crucibles of Leadership*, *Geeks and Geezers* (with Warren G. Bennis), and *Driving Results Through Social Networks* (with Robert L. Cross).

JEFF WEISS is an adjunct professor at the U.S. Military Academy at West Point and a partner at Vantage Partners, a Boston-based consultancy specializing in corporate negotiations and relationship management, where he focuses on sales negotiations and strategic alliances. He is also the author of the *HBR Guide to Negotiating*.

Index

Engage with HBR content the way you want, on any device.

With HBR's new subscription plans, you can access world-renowned **case studies** from Harvard Business School and receive **four free eBooks**. Download and customize prebuilt **slide decks and graphics** from our **Visual Library**. With HBR's archive, top 50 best-selling articles, and five new articles every day, HBR is more than just a magazine.

Subscribe Today
hbr.org/success

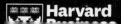

The most important management ideas all in one place.

We hope you enjoyed this book from *Harvard Business Review*. Now you can get even more with HBR's 10 Must Reads Boxed Set. From books on leadership and strategy to managing yourself and others, this 6-book collection delivers articles on the most essential business topics to help you succeed.

HBR's 10 Must Reads Series

The definitive collection of ideas and best practices on our most sought-after topics from the best minds in business.

- Change Management
- Collaboration
- Communication
- Emotional Intelligence
- Innovation
- Leadership
- Making Smart Decisions

- Managing Across Cultures
- Managing People
- Managing Yourself
- Strategic Marketing
- Strategy
- Teams
- The Essentials

hbr.org/mustreads

Buy for your team, clients, or event.
Visit hbr.org/bulksales for quantity discount rates.